THE ENDURING QUEST

By H. A. Overstreet

INFLUENCING HUMAN BEHAVIOR

ABOUT OURSELVES

THE ENDURING QUEST

THE
ENDURING QUEST

A SEARCH FOR A PHILOSOPHY OF LIFE

BY

H. A. OVERSTREET

PROFESSOR AND HEAD OF

DEPARTMENT OF PHILOSOPHY AND PSYCHOLOGY

COLLEGE OF THE CITY OF NEW YORK

THE CHAUTAUQUA PRESS

CHAUTAUQUA, NEW YORK

1931

Copyright, 1931

W · W · NORTON & COMPANY, INC.

70 Fifth Avenue, New York

PRINTED IN THE UNITED STATES OF AMERICA
FOR THE PUBLISHERS BY THE VAIL-BALLOU PRESS

Typography by R. S. Josephy

CONTENTS

v

CONTENTS

Foreword

THERE are two kinds of challenge that life makes to us, the challenge of needs, and the challenge of the "unknowns." In countless ways we respond to the first. The challenge is definite and unmistakable. For the most part we have little choice in the matter. The needs—whether for food, shelter, or for other things—are there to be met. So, marshalling such intelligence as we possess, we set ourselves to meet them.

This is the practical life. It is specific in its demands and clear-cut in its results. When we have achieved the things we need, we can plainly recognize them. There they are before our eyes. We have been obviously successful. If we are more than commonly successful, we exhibit the accumulation of our things as our wealth.

It is folly, of course, to scorn the practical life. One may indeed at times lay too great store by the mere things that one gathers together for prideful display. But on the whole, the more intelligent one is in responding to the urgency of needs, the better. There would seem to be no sense in being so impractical that one starves or freezes to death. Man's history, indeed, records the gradual increase in the power to respond to this first of life's challenges.

But there is also the second. It has by no means the clear-cut objectivity of the first. And when we attempt

to answer the challenge, particularly of those great unknowns of life and the universe that are beyond our
full comprehension, there is nothing that we can set
down before us and say, "These things are ours." It
is for this reason, very often, that response to the challenge of the mysteries of the universe has been regarded
as a rather foolish and useless way of life. It bakes no
bread and butters no toast. It makes no addition to our
computable fortunes. It is "impractical," and therefore
wasteful of good time and energy that might be far
more profitably employed.

And yet there is something important to notice about
the response to this challenge. Animals, apparently, do
not make the response. There is no indication that the
beaver sits on its dam and wonders what life is about.
There are no signs that the busily scurrying ant stops in
its scurrying and reflects upon its environing world.
When we are told, therefore, that we had best not let
ourselves in for such impractical business as bothering
about those things that are apparently beyond our use
and control, it looks suspiciously like asking us to hold
ourselves strictly to the animal level of life.

Man alone has the power to respond to the challenge
of what is beyond specific needs. Is there perhaps something that is significant about this? Man has achieved a
supremacy in the animal kingdom. His mind has, so to
speak, moved beyond the narrow areas of animal life.
Is it perhaps possible that his curious habit of wondering—a kind of wondering that brings no specific results
—may have had no little to do with his release from

the narrow animal into the wider human areas? Or is it perhaps the other way around, that as he gradually released himself from the narrow confines of animalhood, he achieved his more expanded thought-life, the thought-life that can range beyond immediate necessities?

In any event, as a creature that can respond to this second kind of life-challenge, man is unique. If we wish, therefore, to differentiate him most sharply from his animal past and from his present animal fellows, we must apparently do so in terms of this power which is his to respond to the great unknowns of life and the universe. In the possession of this power, man is most uniquely man.

Indeed, there would seem to be good psychological reason for regarding this wider kind of response as of transforming moment in man's life. One can try the experiment in one's own life. To turn for a space of time from intense absorption in particular needs and to let one's mind range freely over the mysteries of existence is to return to one's absorptions a different person. It is hard to describe precisely what happens, but we all know that it does happen. There is a kind of enlargement of oneself, a new power to see things in wider relationships, a calmness and an openness.

This is what one finds in all the master spirits of the ages. One is rather glad that Socrates wasted time on the street-corners of Athens. One rather suspects that something of value came because Spinoza took time off from his grinding of lenses to contemplate the universe.

One feels similarly about all the great artists—Dante, Leonardo, Goethe, Shakespeare, Beethoven, Brahms. These men went beyond the food and shelter needs. They were facing life, death, courage, love, hate, frustration, devotion.

In such as they, one suspects, man has been at his best. Before the majesty of their thought and the sheer beauty of their apprehension, the little businesses of attending to immediate needs, however necessary, seem small and unimportant. Life would require that we get through with these as quickly and effectively as we can in order that we may come to the more real enterprise of living.

That is why poetry, drama, science and philosophy have endured through all the ages. In them man has risen to his more essentially human interest. In them he has emerged from mere animalhood. As Aristotle expresses it, "Nor is it right to follow the advice of people who say that the thoughts of men should not be too high for humanity or the thoughts of mortals too high for mortality; for a man, as far as in him lies, should seek immortality and do all that is in his power to live in accordance with the highest part of his nature." [1]

Thus practical as man in the present century must be, he still has the need to be greatly impractical. He must still go seeking the unattainables. For, curious paradox that it is, in going down to defeat before the unattainables—and he always goes down to defeat—

[1] *Nicomachean Ethics*, Book X.

man achieves, in the world of the attainables, his greater victories.

In this book we are holding ourselves altogether to the second of life's challenges. No apology is needed for that, only the conviction that we come to the most authentic in ourselves as we go forth to that which is immeasurably greater than ourselves. We in our twentieth century, because we are still man, carry on the enduring quest. We seek for a significance which, no doubt, we shall only partly find. But we seek it nevertheless.

I should like to dedicate this book to a small group of men and women of the New School for Social Research who foregathered once a week of a late afternoon to discuss the lectures which I was then giving on *Life and Destiny*. As a matter of fact, what we discussed was almost everything except the lectures. We never quite knew where we were going to start nor in what direction we were to advance, but in the end we always seemed to touch some rim of the great central issues of life. I am not sure that we ever solved anything. In fact, I am quite sure that we did not. But this appeared to leave us in no despair. Indeed, we seemed to discover with increasing certitude that man does not live by proofs alone, but by many an unexpected insight which he achieves on the way.

It is those insights which I recall, many of them leaping suddenly out of some chance remark. This book is in large measure a kind of effort to think them through into some manner of coherent synthesis.

Very deeply and persistently, we seek a philosophy of life. Our existence, for the most part, is a kind of puzzle picture which we feel that we must in some way put together. We have, indeed, a fairly convinced notion that we shall never quite get it all together, but, as we fit piece to piece, there is a curious delight in each momentary triumph. And despite our notion to the contrary, there is always the hope that, by a stroke of good fortune, we shall come upon some master clue which will sweep the thing into an illuminating unity.

We are particularly hopeful in these present days. A new spirit of inquiry has been awakened, a new movement of thought is on the way. Much of what has been accepted, both philosophically and scientifically, is now no longer accepted. Both science and philosophy are moving away from old positions. It is doubtless true that this century will yet witness the formulation of a view of life and the universe that in many respects will be different from any that has hitherto been held. The hope is that it will not only be different, but truer.

I wish to make special acknowledgment to my colleague, Dr. Edward W. Strong, and his wife, Gertrude Strong, who patiently submitted themselves to the hearing of the entire manuscript and who made invaluable suggestions. They are, of course, not to be regarded as necessarily in full agreement with all the views expressed in this book. I wish also to thank the several authors quoted, and their publishers, for permission to use their material.

Part One

REORIENTATING OURSELVES

The world is not a "prison house," but a kind of spiritual kindergarten, where millions of bewildered infants are trying to spell God with the wrong blocks.

EDWIN ARLINGTON ROBINSON

Chapter I

THE SCIENTIFIC UPHEAVAL

REVISED CONCEPTIONS OF THE PHYSICAL UNIVERSE

PERHAPS the most momentous thing that has occurred in recent decades, so far as our beliefs about the world are concerned, has been the downfall of accepted certainties in physics. It is a momentous happening for the reason that physics is the science which, more than any other, has, in recent decades, set the pattern for our intelligent thinking. Nor has it done this merely among the few highly trained scientists. Its influence has extended to the increasingly large number of well read people, so that today one is far more apt to find among such individuals those who believe in a world of atoms than in a world of angels and planetary spirits. One is far more apt to find among them a conviction that the mind is a function of the brain, and that when the brain dies the mind dies with it, than the older conviction that the mind is a spiritual entity which goes independently on its immortal way. Finally, one is more likely to discover among them a belief in the inexorable and purposeless processes of matter than a belief in a guiding Deity who is responsive to human petition. In one way and another, in short, the modern trend of intelligent thought, as influenced by

15

physical science, has been toward a materialistic conception of the universe and of life.

As one reviews the history of man's curiously misconceived gods and goddesses, demons, spirits, and the rest, one is led to feel that this movement toward a materialistic conception of the universe, however mistaken, has been of real value. Most of the traditional thinking of men has suffered from the infantile fallacy of anthropomorphism, the fallacy, namely, of conceiving the forces of nature in the image of the human being. Even in ancient days, the Greek philosopher, Xenophanes, expressed his scorn of this procedure: "If horses and lions had hands to paint, they would have painted their gods after the nature of themselves: horses would have painted horse-gods and lions lion-gods." To people the heavens with creatures like themselves may have been a comfort to men's fears and an aid to their vanity, but it did not stimulate them to a serious effort toward understanding and controlling their world. The long and arduous process of scientific observation and experiment tended, in the main, to correct this anthropomorphic folly. The centuries of brilliant scientific investigation, following the first researches of Galileo, Copernicus, Kepler, Huyghens, and the other pioneers, culminated in a view of the universe in which there was no place for naïve spiritual entities. The universe was matter and the movements of matter.

Nevertheless, when physics started its modern career a little over three hundred years ago, it had no intention of displacing the religious or spiritual view of life and the world. All it then sought was freedom to think of physical things in ways untrammeled by theology. It granted the right of theology to the spiritual realm. It asked only to be permitted, without dogmatic hindrance, to explore the physical world.

But we remember the story. As physical discoveries followed close upon the heels of one another, opening up a universe far vaster than, and, in its processes, far different from what had hitherto been conceived, the description of the world given by the religious writers was increasingly seen to be without warrant. Religious leaders, however, loath to yield any part of the world's domain to the new scientists, kept insisting upon the facts as described in the revealed Word. The earth, they stoutly maintained, was the center of the solar system; the sun moved around the earth; outside the earth were the circles of the planets; and outside them all was the circle of Heaven. At the center of the earth was the place of fiery punishment.

The discoveries of the scientists went counter to one after another of these descriptions. What is more, they were verified by indubitable observation and experiment. Therefore, the religious assertions about the physical world increasingly lost their authority. When finally Newton gathered up the previous observations of the celestial physicists into one grand synthesis, the traditional religious conception of the physical world-order met a crucial defeat. To be sure, Newton himself, a deeply pious man, felt that his mechanical conception of the universe in nowise encroached upon the spiritual truths of religion. God was to him a Spirit Invisible, and man was the son of God. Nevertheless, the authority of that written Source from which all truth had hitherto sprung was greatly weakened.

It was still more weakened when, in the middle of the nineteenth century, the Darwinian hypothesis—following in the spirit of heretical geologists—displaced the biblical account of creation. This was an even more crucial overturn than the Newtonian one. Newton had left man untouched. Man could still, despite the grand regularity of the physical universe, be conceived as a very special object of God's concern, created in His image and destined to a life everlasting. But when Darwin showed man to be only a rather humble descendant of the ape, that belief had of necessity to go into the discard. Man was, as it were, one with the brutes, not one with the angels.

Thus by the second half of the nineteenth century the authority of the religious account of the universe had been so disqualified that the minds of the more intelligent were ripe for a new kind of truth. And this truth was now apparently ready to hand. For that science of physics which had begun in its small way by dropping weights from the Tower of Pisa and by making laborious observations of stars and planets, had at last, through the successive achievements of three centuries, become the authoritative science. Men turned to it as to a source of verifiable truth.

And indeed physics seemed in full measure to justify men's confidence, for the laws of the universe which it formulated hung together with so exquisite a nicety and so inescapable a universality that there was nothing to do save to accept them as a veritable account of things.

The truth which physics seemed to reveal, however, was of a very different kind from that which had been taught by the religious leaders. It was a view of a completely mechanical universe. The parts of that universe were atoms. Its laws were those of atomic movement. Reality, in short, was masses in motion.

So convincing was the picture drawn by the triumphant physics of the nineteenth century that it was accepted by an increasing body of thinkers, despite the fact that it delivered to man a smashing blow. For, when taken as a complete account of reality, it deprived man altogether of his most cherished possession—the belief in his own significance. It reduced him to a transient combination of atomic particles. It denied any enduring validity to his mind. His mind, in fact, because it fell outside the range of physical measurement, was a negligible kind of superfluity in the universe, an "epiphenomenon" —"epi" meaning that it did not really belong to the essential atomic order of things.

It was a hard blow to take; but man, being a creature curiously devoted to his truth-seeking processes, bravely took the blow. In increasing numbers, particularly among the scientists, he embraced materialism as a philosophy of life. For materialism was the philosophy which seemed inevitably to follow from a science which could find nothing that was basically real save atoms and the movements of atoms.

The Scientific Upheaval

That was the situation in which most well read individuals found themselves in the latter part of the nineteenth century. And there seemed every reason to believe that they would remain in that situation.

Then something happened. It happened in the last years of the century. A discovery was made, of a new kind of ray. This does not sound particularly cataclysmic, yet it suddenly shook all that carefully reared structure of physical hypotheses, which had seemed to be of so enduring a nature, to the ground.

We can do no better than to describe this swift overturn in the words of one of the eye witnesses, himself one of the outstanding scientists of the world.[1]

"The transition from the old to the new mode of thought in physics was probably made as dramatically in my case as in that of anyone in the world; for I was in the fortunate position of having entered the field just three years before the end of the complete dominance of nineteenth century modes of thought. In those three years I had the privilege of personally meeting and hearing lectures by the most outstanding creators of nineteenth century physics—Kelvin, Helmholtz, Boltzman, Poincaré, Rayleigh, Van't Hoff, Michelson, Ostwald, Lorentz—every one of whom I met and heard between 1892 and 1896. In one of these lectures I listened with rapt attention to the expression of a point

[1] Millikan, R. A., *Evolution in Science and Religion*, pp. 7–11 (Yale University Press).

of view which was undoubtedly held by most of them—
indeed, by practically all physicists of that epoch; for it
had been given expression more than once by the most
distinguished men of the nineteenth century.

"The speaker had reviewed, first, the establishment
and definite proof of the principles of mechanics during
the seventeenth and eighteenth centuries culminating in
La Place's great *Mécanique céleste;* then he had turned
to the wonderfully complete verification of the wave
theory of light by Young and Fresnel, between 1800
and 1830, experiments which laid secure foundations for
the later structure known as the physics of the ether, one
of the most beautiful products of nineteenth century
thinking and experimenting; then he had traced the development in the middle of the century of the generalization of all science, the principle of the conservation of
energy; then he had spoken of the establishment in the
first two decades of the second half of the century of the
second law of thermodynamics, the principle of entropy
or of the degradation of energy, and finally of the development by Maxwell of the electromagnetic theory
and its experimental verification by Hertz in 1886, only
seven years earlier than the date of the lecture. This
theory abolished in all particulars except wave length
the distinction between light and radiant heat and long
electromagnetic waves, all these phenomena being included under the general head of the physics of the
ether.

"Then, summarizing this wonderfully complete, well-
verified, and apparently all-inclusive set of laws and

principles into which it seemed that all physical phenomena must forever fit, the speaker concluded that it
was probable that all the great discoveries in physics had
already been made and that future progress was to be
looked for, not in bringing to light qualitatively new
phenomena, but rather in making more exact quantitative measurements upon old phenomena.

"Just a little more than one year later, and before I
had ceased pondering over the afore-mentioned lecture, I was present in Berlin on Christmas Eve, 1895,
when Professor Roentgen presented to the German
Physical Society his first X-ray photographs. Some of
them were of the bones of the hand, others of coins and
keys photographed through the opaque walls of a leather
pocket-book, all clearly demonstrating that he had found
some strange new rays which had the amazing property
of penetrating as opaque an object as the human body
and revealing on a photographic plate the skeleton of a
living person.

"Here was a completely new phenomenon—a qualitatively new discovery and one having nothing to do
with the principles of exact measurement. *As I listened
and as the world listened, we all began to see that the
nineteenth century physicists had taken themselves a
little too seriously, that we had not come quite as near
sounding the depths of the universe, even in the matter
of fundamental physical principles, as we thought we
had.*"

Then followed discovery on discovery. In the succeeding year, the process of radio-activity was revealed. Be-

cause of the discovery of what was apparently happening inside those supposedly hard little entities, the atoms, they were now subjected to new exploration. They had been thought, following the figure of the famed billiard balls, to be impenetrable little masses impinging on other impenetrable little masses. In 1899, Sir J. J. Thomson isolated in the atom the ultimate unit of negative electricity, the electron. From that it was but a short distance to the overthrow of the old atomic view and the substitution of a new hypothesis which changed the hard little masses into centers of electric energy. In 1900, Max Planck, of Berlin University, discovered what is now known as the *quantum*, the minute unit of radiant action shot off by radiant bodies and even by dark bodies. In 1901, the further discovery was made that the mass of one of these sub-atoms, the electron, is not fixed, as one would expect it to be, but that it increases as it approaches the speed of light. With that discovery went the old reliable principle of the conservation of matter.

What, now, was matter? No one really knew. Between electrons, protons, *quanta*, the co-variation of acceleration and mass, the thing that had seemed plainest of all realities—good solid matter—the most trustworthy of all possible realities, and indeed the rock-bottom reality, vanished into a vast perplexity.

"The childish mechanical conceptions of the nineteenth century," Millikan goes on to say, "are now grotesquely inadequate."

And now, in recent years, has come another striking change. Planck's discovery of the unit of radiation in

1900 started a process of thinking, the end of which is not yet in sight. Broadly speaking it showed up the inadequacy of the wave theory of light and substituted a view more nearly in line with the older corpuscular or discontinuity theory. Nevertheless, at the present time, both theories are invoked by physicists as circumstances require, despite the fact that the two are in basic conflict with each other. What is most striking about the new quantum theory and what is of most interest to us in our present inquiry is the curious turn which the recent developments of it have given to our conception of scientific knowledge. Hitherto scientists have felt that the possibilities of exploring the world are endless. It is now shown that there is an actual limit beyond which scientific research cannot go. The contention is based on the fact that seeing is a process that involves an interaction of light rays between the seer and the object seen. When the object to be seen is as minute as an electron, the disturbance caused by the act of seeing is such that no accurate observation can be made. Thus there is a point beyond which observation cannot go, and since meaning is possible only where there can be observation, there is a realm of nature which is and must remain completely meaningless. In this meaningless realm, the laws which operate in the world we know have no meaning. The basic law of all laws to the scientist is the law of causality. But now, by the reduction of the sub-observable world to meaninglessness, the law of causality is denied entrance, and we are left with a realm of nature in which the law of causality itself does not operate.

Here, then, is the completest breakdown of the mechanistic structure that seemed so secure in the nineteenth-century physics. Just where these new conceptions will now lead no one seems as yet to know. As Eddington remarks: "It would probably be wiser to nail up over the door of the new quantum theory a notice, 'Structural alterations in progress— No admittance except on business,' and particularly to warn the doorkeeper to keep out prying philosophers." [2]

The New Outlook

Reviewing all this, we can appreciate Millikan's further word,[3] said in the generous spirit of a true scientist: "We have learned to work with new satisfaction, new hope, and a new enthusiasm because there is still so much that we do not understand, and because, instead of having it all pigeonholed, as they thought they had, we have found in our lifetime more new relations in physics than have come to light in all the preceding ages put together, and because the stream of discovery as yet shows no signs of abatement. . . . We can still look with a sense of wonder and mystery and reverence upon the fundamental elements as they have been *partially* revealed to us in this century." [4]

We need only add to this the words of another scien-

[2] *The Nature of the Physical World*, p. 211 (Macmillan). See also Jeans, Sir James, *The Universe Around Us*, pp. 115 ff. (Macmillan), Bridgman, P. W., "The New Vision of Science" (Harper's Magazine, March, 1929).

[3] Millikan, R. A., *Evolution in Science and Religion*, p. 27.

[4] Italics ours.

tist to make the account complete. They come from the pen of J. S. Haldane, one of England's outstanding biologists: "Materialism, once a scientific theory, is now the fatalistic creed of thousands, but materialism is nothing better than a superstition on the same level as belief in witches and devils."

"What does it all mean?" writes Millikan,[5] after recounting the manner in which discoveries have led on to other discoveries. "Simply that there is an interrelatedness, a unity, a oneness about the whole of nature, and yet still an amazing mystery."

Where there is an amazing mystery, it now seems ill-advised to be certain about things. The old confident nineteenth-century materialism, among the alert scientists, lies in ruins. Modern physicists are not even bothering about that older materialism, save, with as great an expedition as possible, to remove the débris. They are at some new kind of building up of hypotheses. What the new factors in those hypotheses are to be, and what form they are to take, are puzzles whose solution lies in the lap of the future.

[5] "Alleged Sins of Science" (Scribner's Magazine, February, 1930).

Chapter II

A FALSE WAY OF THINKING

THE FALLACY OF ABSTRACTION

WHILE this vigor of reconstruction and new research among the physicists is expending itself in various ways, we may pause for a moment to take stock of what was basically wrong with that old confidence as it shaped itself into a curiously self-defeating view of the universe. Fundamentally, it implied a wrong way of thinking. Because this wrong way of thinking is very much in evidence among us and constantly gets us into difficulties out of which we must later more or less ignominiously extricate ourselves, it is worth examining.

Here again let us consult a scientist—for the heartening thing today is that it does not require a philosopher crying in the wilderness to tell the world what was wrong with the materialism that grew out of the nineteenth-century science. The scientists themselves are telling the story. One of the most penetrating of these is Eddington.

In an illuminating chapter on the method of science and on the relation which that method bears to our search for reality,[1] Eddington begins by noting the dif-

[1] "The Domain of Science," in *Science, Religion and Reality*, edited by Joseph Needham, pp. 189 ff. (Macmillan).

ference between the point of view of the common man
and that of the scientist:

"The learned physicist and the man in the street were
standing together on the threshold about to enter a room.

"The man in the street moved forward without
trouble, planted his foot on a solid unyielding plank at
rest before him, and entered.

"The physicist was faced with an intricate problem.
To make any movement he must shove against the atmosphere, which presses with a force of fourteen pounds
on every square inch of his body. He must land on a
plank travelling at twenty miles a second round the sun
—a fraction of a second earlier or later the plank would
be miles away from the chosen spot. He must do this
whilst hanging from a round planet head outward into
space, and with a wind of ether blowing at no one knows
how many miles a second through every interstice of his
body. He reflects too that the plank is not what it appears to be—a continuous support for his weight. The
plank is mostly emptiness; very sparsely scattered in
that emptiness are myriads of electric charges dashing
about at great speeds but occupying at any moment less
than a billionth part of the volume which the plank
seems to fill continuously. It is like stepping on a swarm
of flies. Will he not slip through? No, if he makes the
venture, he falls for an instant till an electron hits him
and gives him a boost up again; he falls again, and is
knocked upwards by another electron; and so on. The
net result is that he neither slips through the swarm nor

is bombarded up to the ceiling, but is kept about steady in his shuttlecock fashion. Or rather, it is not certain but highly probable that he remains steady; and if, unfortunately, he should sink through the floor or hit the ceiling, the occurrence would not be a violation of the laws of nature but a rare coincidence.

"By careful calculation of these and other conditions the physicist may reach a solution of the problem of entering a room; and, if he is fortunate enough to avoid mathematical blunders, he will prove satisfactorily that the feat can be accomplished in the manner already adopted by his ignorant companion. Happily even a learned physicist has usually some sense of proportion; and it is probable that for this occasion he put out of mind scientific truths about astronomical motions, the constitution of planks and the laws of probability, and was content to follow the same crude conception of his task that presented itself to the mind of his unscientific colleague."

Awarding a Double Prize

To whom, it might be asked, should the prize be awarded for holding the true view of the situation? Should we laud the common man for being so untroubled by all this phantasmagoria of mathematics and electric charges that he goes ahead with nonchalant ignorance and steps on the plank? Or should we laud—even though we pity—the much worried scientist who must watch his every step and add his figures meticulously lest he slip through a hole in the cosmos? Eddington concludes that we should award the prize to both. They are both right —each in his own way.

There is a curious tendency, however, to say that the scientist is right, even though the common man may be quite successful and may live a considerably less harried life. When the common man tells us that he sees no electrons, feels none, that so far as he can apprehend there are no holes in the plank, that, on the contrary, the plank is a good solid piece of walkable timber, we tend to smile in superiority. The common man does not know his science. As a matter of real fact (note the word "real"), the plank is electrons and protons.

This same attitude manifests itself in other instances. An individual is listening to music. "Beautiful," he says. "But," we say, "do you really know about music? Come into our laboratory and we shall show you the vibrations you are now experiencing. Music is mathematical physics. Unless one knows mathematical physics one cannot know music." If, now, the individual, being thus admonished, accepts, he will have a different experience. He will see a whole range of figures, each figure indicating a tone's vibrations. "But where is the music?" he might ask. Again we tend to be a little superior. He simply does not know his science.

Eddington, on the contrary, does not exhibit any such superiority. "There is one conception of our physical environment appropriate to scientific inquiry," he writes, "and another conception appropriate to the ordinary daily contacts." The significant thing is that both are

appropriate, and both, therefore—each in its own way
—true. He goes on to illustrate what he means. "The
scientist," he says, "looks at the world through a magni-
fying glass." That, of course, as he points out, is one
possible way in which to look at it. "Magnification gives
us the world as we might suppose it to appear to creatures built on a smaller scale than ourselves, capable
of appreciating smaller distances, shorter moments of
time." We can, if we wish, imagine ourselves in the position of microscopic creatures, and by so doing we shall
probably achieve much useful information. But, he goes
on significantly to add: "Do we really get nearer to the
truth of things by changing from the point of view of a
man to that of a microbe?"

The answer is that by so doing we get *a* truth about
things. There actually are those microscopic relations.
There are those atoms and those sub-atoms. It is exceedingly useful for us to know them. But there are also
other relations and entities that are not at all microscopic.
And it is doubtless useful for us to know them also.
Thus, to return to the musical illustration, the relation
of musical sounds to an individual who is emotionally
stirred by them is precisely as real as the relation of these
same sounds to the recording instrument of the physicist.
One takes one's choice. Or better, if one is wise, one
takes many choices. One allows, in short, for many points
of view, and one does not believe that one has actually
compassed the reality of anything until one has apprehended it from all points of view that are humanly
possible.

How Do We Know an Individual?

We may illustrate this from a slightly different angle of approach. Here, for example is an individual, Richard Jones. You have just been introduced to him. A swift glance, and you have made an estimate. If you are very proud of your so-called intuitive powers, you will believe that in that swift glance you have taken in the real man. You have made an appropriate judgment about him. The judgment you make in this particular case is that Richard Jones is a sulky person not worth knowing.

It happened, however, that Richard Jones, that day, was suffering the pains of the damned. He had a toothache, and as he was introduced there was a glum look on his face that boded good to no one. Next week, you may meet him again and be agreeably surprised to find the same Richard Jones a delightfully genial, sympathetic, and altogether charming creature. If, however, you insist that, for yourself, a single contact with an individual is enough, you may persist in holding to your initial judgment, believing that, all appearances to the contrary, the real Richard Jones is a sulky person.

Obviously you come to know the real individual only as you know him from many points of view. To know him from the bridge-table point of view is not enough, nor from the dance-floor point of view, nor from the business-office point of view. If you know him only from a single point of view, you may easily go wrong. You may, indeed, be right about what you find from that point of view; but what you find is not yet enough to give you the fulness of the life that is this individual. Thus, we often say, if you wish to know a person really, go camping with him, or marry him. Camping and marriage supposedly provide one with a sufficient number of angles of approach to make possible a judgment that is fairly adequate.

The Fallacy of Abstraction

The true object of our awareness, in short—whether it be a Richard Jones, a symphony, or the universe—must be the synthesis of all possible points of view. As long as one regards an object only from one or two points of view, one's knowledge of it is abstract. The etymology of the word abstract is in this connection illuminating: *abs-trahere*—to draw away. Knowledge is abstract when something has been drawn away from the fulness of its reality and made to stand by itself. Thus the mathematical account of music is abstract inasmuch as the musical experience, while indeed including the mathematical relations, includes far more. Knowledge of anything, to be fully true, must be concrete. Again the etymology is significant: *con-crescere*—to grow together.

To reject any natural point of view as wrong is, therefore, itself wrong. One notes this particular error committed time and again throughout the history of thought. The Eleatic philosophers in Greece turned from change and multiplicity. Because they could make no logical system out of them, they brushed them aside. Only movelessness, they concluded, is real. But the Eleatics were simply taking the unreal path of abstraction. They were moving away from the fulness of experience rather than toward it. A whole scheme of life in the Orient has apparently been reared upon this method of abstraction. This life of desire and activity, say certain Hindu philosophers, is *Maya*, illusion. Reality is found by slipping away from the world of illusion into the moveless reality of Brahm. So we find, among those who hold this view, a going apart from ordinary activities, a sitting in undisturbed meditation, in that meditation reducing the area of experience to the smallest dimensions, until the conscious life becomes as emptied as possible of all details. The sage who sits looking at his navel, endlessly repeating the same word, is, by a process of self-hypnosis, inducing a mental blankness that, instead of being an approach to the fulness of reality, is simply an escape from the multiplicity of experience. He is, in short, achieving an abstraction. He believes, to be sure, that he is achieving the ultimate reality, but if the foregoing is correct, he is finding not the fulness of reality, but the emptiness of unreality.

A like fallacious procedure prevailed among the mediæval ascetics. They rejected one entire side of human experience—the bodily—as unworthy. They drew away from it with a kind of horror. The life of the spirit was to them the only true reality. As a result of their abstract process they invested the word "spirit" with so thin and lifeless a meaning that even today the use of the word—as likewise the adjective "spiritual"—is involved in grave ambiguities and leads to the suspicion that one is again seeking reality by withdrawing from a very real part of it. Asceticism, in short, wherever it exists, commits the fallacy of regarding a part or aspect as the whole. This has sometimes been described as the process of "hypostatizing an abstraction," in other words, making the non-self-sufficient into the self-sufficient. More recently, the process has been described by Whitehead as the "fallacy of misplaced concreteness." The ascetic, searching for the concrete, thought that he had found it in spirit detached from body. But he had misplaced the concrete. Instead of finding the concrete where it really is, in the fulness of experience, he believed mistakenly that he had found it in a partial aspect of experience.

What Physics Really Does

It may seem a little strange to place philosophical physicists of the nineteenth century in the same category with Hindu and mediæval ascetics. Nevertheless the relationship is a true one. The nineteenth-century physicists were, of course, making notable contributions to human knowledge. But an understandable thing happened. For a good many centuries man had sought reality. It was natural to suppose that reality would be found in one or another special region of existence—precisely as the ascetic tried to find it in the special region of spirit. Thus, when the atom was discovered, it was supposed to be reality *par excellence*. Everything else was conceived to be derivative. Some parts of experience, indeed, were not even explainably derivative, because they showed no traces of this fundamental reality. Thoughts and emotions were of this kind. The laboratory physicists could make nothing of these baffling psychological phenomena. They took them into their laboratories; but no single thought or emotion ever delivered itself of an atom. Apparently, then, these phenomena, for some unexplained reason, did not belong to the real world which they had discovered.

Eddington again casts light upon this situation, expressing the attitude of contemporary scientists: "The external world is . . . a synthesis of appearances from all possible points of view." When Eddington says "all possible" he means precisely what these two words mean. One possible point of view is that of the microscopic eye aforesaid. Through the microscopic eye we get our atoms and sub-atoms. But another possible point of view is that of the conscious observer. Physics disregards the second point of view, he would say, not because it is unreal, and therefore unworthy, but because physics can work more effectively by carefully restricting its inquiry. To say, however, that what physics discovers, when it isolates itself from all except this special, microscopic point of view, is the exclusively true reality, is to commit the fallacy of abstraction. No, the true reality is the synthesis of all possible points of view.

As Eddington shows, modern physics has made one of its most striking successes by abandoning to a certain extent one of its older attitudes of abstraction and accepting, even in its restricted field, this "principle of synthesis."

For example, the revolution in our thought effected by Einstein was brought about by departing from the abstract point of view of the old Newtonian physics and trying to envisage the physical universe from all possible space-time points of view. Thus, in the Newtonian way of thinking, space and movement were described from the earth point of view. Einstein asked the simple question: What will happen if we regard the spacial universe from the point of view of observers on different heavenly bodies? As a result, the old, simple, earth-focussed mechanics was expanded into the far more "real" mechanics of relativity.

Is Exact Knowledge the Only Kind of Knowledge?

Now the distinguishing feature of science is that it aims at *exactness*. Exactness is found where the matters in question can be reduced to mathematical terms. It might be said that science is the search for mathematical reality.

But a question suggests itself. When one has found the mathematical relations involved in a thing has one fully described that thing? For example, the weight of Kant's *Critique of Pure Reason* may be the same as the weight of a burglar's blackjack. Are they, then, the same? If we are simply interested in weighing things, we shall stop there. But if we are interested in knowing things, we shall of course have to go much farther. So, the fundamental measurable elements—atoms—are the same in a man and an amœba. Are the two creatures identical in their reality? Again, if we are interested simply in finding the measurable elements of things, we shall stop with the measurable identity; but if we are interested in knowing things, we must go much farther.

This is a crucial point. It is sometimes said that science is the sole road to knowledge and that any advance to the truth save by way of science is not to be tolerated. It all depends upon what we mean by science. If we take the meaning that most competent scientists hold, namely, that science is exact knowledge, or at least aims at exact knowledge, and if we realize that exactness can be achieved only when the matters in question are reduced to mathematical terms, it is obvious that to hold ourselves solely to science would immeasurably impoverish our knowledge. It would be—following Eddington once more—like supposing that the numbers attached to the names of telephone subscribers gave an adequate account of each subscriber. These numbers are exact, and they are very necessary. They transform an otherwise maddening complication of relationships into a triumphantly simple scheme. But, if one is himself a subscriber, would one not be a trifle loath to believe that the particular combination of numbers placed opposite his name not only exactly but completely expressed the reality of his individual self?

"The subscriber is an entity with various aspects; he is (1) a number, (2) a plughole, (3) a voice, and even (4) a human being. In the first and second aspects (which are the aspects with which the operator is most concerned), subscriber No. 1357 may be dissected into digits, 1, 3, 5, 7, or into board 1, section 3, row 5, column 7. This dissection is of importance in explaining some of the mysterious properties of subscribers—for example, why Lady Blank, No. 1357, is so often confused with the chimney-sweep, No. 1397, a phenomenon not explicable by reference to the undissected aspects of these subscribers. Again, it explains why on one occasion the voices for which the first digit is 2 all became silent simultaneously. The telephone operator might well get into the habit of thinking that subscribers were entities composed of four constituents, because this analysis is true of the aspects which he studies; but we cannot analyse a human being into four parts corresponding to the digits of his telephone number." [2]

We seem equally justified in suspecting that neither can human beings—nor any other beings for that matter—be fully described in terms of their atomic parts, parts, indeed, which are doubtless indispensably there, but which are far from being the full reality.

And so the fallacy of that nineteenth-century thought is obvious. It selected an important aspect of reality, and then failed to realize that it was only an aspect. It tried to make us believe that all other aspects of ourselves— thoughts, desires, loves, hates, plannings and purposings —were either just so much unreality or reducible to the physical elements. Materialism was the view which reared this falsity of abstraction into a philosophy of life.

But, as we indicated in the previous chapter, mate-

[2] *Ibid.*, p. 201.

rialism, for all alert minds, is discredited. We can see now why it should be discredited. It was the result of a false way of thinking. True thinking will seek not one point of view, but all possible points of view. It will go the way, not of abstraction, but of the completest kind of synthesis.

The Method of Many Points of View

In a recent interview, Einstein is reported to have said: [3] "Music and physical research originate in different sources, but they are interrelated as to their common aim, which is the desire to express the unknown. Their reactions are different, but their results are supplementary." Probably nothing could be more salutary than the emphasis of this point of view. It is one which approaches its world with a certain comprehensiveness of understanding. It is not a one-track view. It suspects that, whatever form experience may take, there is, in each form, something that is, in its way, a clue to reality. Thus it has no lordly scorn. It does not, because it is overimpressed with matter, relegate mind to a bloodless realm of epiphenomena. Nor, overimpressed with mind, does it wave body aside as unworthy of human concern. It does not exalt science at the expense of art, nor art at the expense of science. Every real way of experiencing life is to it a way that has significance; and by regarding fully what each experience has to say for itself, it expects to achieve the fullest possible understanding.

[3] *New York Times*, September 14, 1930.

Science is now entering upon that new way of understanding. The old days of dogmatic abstraction are doubtless well over. Whatever be the nature of the new universe we shall build, it is a fair guess that it will not again—at least for a long time—be constructed out of some single element which we have happily discovered and about which we have become hugely excited. We shall probably do a good deal of traveling around the universe, looking at it from this side and from that, before we get emphatic about saying what the universe or what life really is.

Chapter III

MATTER AND LIFE APPROACH
EACH OTHER

CONTRIBUTIONS OF THE NEW PHYSICS

WE have noted the series of discoveries that changed our older view of the atom. That older view was peculiarly baffling. In the midst of life it left us, as it were, with non-life as the sole authentic reality. For the upshot of the theory was an insistence on the superior reality of a world of inert masses. Inert masses were the *real* reality. Life, indeed, was apparently here, but how it could possibly have come out of those inert, impenetrable masses seemed to be insoluble. And how this still more vivid and active reality, mind, could have come seemed likewise completely unexplainable.

The universe had been turned upside down. The living was thought to have been generated out of the non-living, instead of the non-living, or inert, being thought of as a passing or partial phase of the living. Regarded logically, of course, the latter would seem to be the altogether tenable view to hold. For it is not difficult to conceive of a certain inertness in living things. We find it among ourselves. Despite our varying activities, we form habits that remain more or less fixed throughout our lifetime. Indeed we cannot conceive of a complete and utter fluidity. Where all things flow, nothing flows, since flow must be measured against at least a relative fixity.

Thus inertness can have a conceivable place in the realm of the living. But to generate the living out of the non-living seems to go beyond all possible conceiving. It is *creatio ex nihilo*.

If now we regard the work of the new physics, we note that this former, apparently illogical, position has been abandoned. The inert atom has been changed into a powerful center of energy.

The New Type of Atom

When we examine these minute, atomic centers of energy, we discover in them a remarkable organization of activity. The new physics, to be sure, presents merely a theory. It has never been able to penetrate these centers of energy so as adequately to behold what is going on within them. But, through experiments of the greatest refinement and skill, it has been able to get circumstantial evidence of a kind that goes far toward substantiating the new views.

All of that evidence points to the fact that each atom is in some respects very like an organism. Thus it has a definable structure and unity of behavior. All the parts within it act, not as a kind of loose aggregate, but as subject to the configuration of the whole. The hydrogen electron, for example, is supposed to move in regular ways about its nucleus, the proton. And it makes as much difference in the atomic world whether there is one nucleus to move around, or two, or more, and whether electrons move in certain orbits or in others, as it makes a difference in the organic world whether the genes are those of a rabbit or of a man.

There are, in short, orders of atoms, as there are orders of organic beings. One does not expect a potato-bug to change its essential structure and become a fruit-fly. Neither does one expect a hydrogen atom to become a nitrogen atom. The atom, in short, has a self-maintaining power. If self-maintenance is the first law of life, and structural organization is the first indispensable condition of life, the atom at least has these.

Also there are simpler atoms and more complex ones, stabler atoms and atoms less stable. In fact to regard the world of atoms is to regard no monotonous world of sameness but one of distinguishable differences. We are aware of these differences in the organic world because we see them with our eyes. Thus we easily recognize different plant and animal forms. On the other hand, we cannot see the atoms with our normal vision. We simply surmise that they are there, and so for most of us they are merely an indistinguishable mass of little somethings that go through their more or less important movements in ways that practically never arouse us to observation. But the physicists and chemists, with their microscopic eyes and their power of inference, are aware of more than this. They know, for example, that there is an individuality of quality about a nitrogen atom that is as marked as the individuality of quality that we observe in any plant or animal. Thus there is a nitrogen order, a hydrogen order, a helium order, precisely as, in the organic world, there is an order of conifers and of crustacea. And while these orders may mingle—as they do in the world of the organic—they never really lose their identity.

Now there are a number of behaviors connected with organic life that atoms seem not to exhibit. Thus, for example, there is a sexual process of reproduction in the animal order that seems not to be observed in the atomic order. But this same sexual process is not observed in all animal orders. There may be life without sexual reproduction, as in the case of those animal forms that propagate by fission. Thus it is illegitimate to deny life to that which does not reproduce itself in one particular way. How the atoms reproduce themselves, or whether they do, is a mooted question and still far from being settled. But they at least seem to have the power, as aforesaid, of maintaining their identities and of acting in terms of a describable structural unity.

Dead Matter Disappears

When we observe the life processes themselves, we note something that is singularly like the atomic processes. Life begins in the cell. But the cell is no undifferentiated mass. It, too, is a structure. It has its nucleus and its surrounding bodies. Out of the powerful energizing of these the life grows and maintains itself. Such self-maintenance and growth are accomplished by an infinitely complex interaction between the active cells and other energy-centers in its world. Thus, for example, the cell—which is itself a chemical structure—combines with other chemical elements in its environment. We say, roughly speaking, that it takes in foods. Also, it transforms these into other combinations, likewise chemical. We call this the process or activity of metabolism. And it rejects certain parts of itself—casts them out of the orbit of its life—so that they take their places in other environmental orbits. We call this elimination.

Life, in short, is a complicated and multitudinous process that goes on within minute centers of organized energy.

Now we can, if we wish—following this train of thought—say that all life is chemical, or that all that is chemical is life. It does not matter now in which way we speak. However, it mattered a great deal in the last century, for then the chemical centers were inert masses, and to call life chemical was, in effect, to call it non-living. Now, however, the chemical elements have at least the two chief characteristics of life—self-maintenance and structural activity.

Matter Approaches Life

"The old contradictory notion of dead matter as the vehicle and carrier of life must disappear in the light of our new knowledge. The difference between matter and life is no longer measured by the distance between absolute passivity on the one hand, and activity on the other—a distance so great as to constitute an impassable gulf in thought. The difference between them is merely a difference in the character of their activities. So far from matter being pure inertia or passivity, it is in reality a mass of seething, palpitating energies and activities. Its very dead-weight simply means the push of inner activity. . . . From the new point of view, the inertia of matter is simply the result of the movement of Nature's internal energy; its apparent passivity is merely the other side of its real activity. Matter is nothing but concentrated structural energy, energy stereotyped into structure. As space contracts with velocity, so mass or the inertia of matter increases through that contraction, and both the mass of matter and its quality of inertia or passiveness are therefore mere variable dependent aspects of Nature's high-speed energies. From this point of view matter is but a form of energy, concentrated by its exceeding velocity, and structured to appear massive or substantial. The very nature of the physical universe is activity or Action." [1]

The Atomic Elements Change

There is a further vista that has opened to us. In former days we were accustomed to think of organic species as fixed types, created at the beginning of the world and remaining as they were created in perpetuity. Now we believe that organic species go through a process of evolution.

[1] Smuts, J. C., *Holism*, p. 51 (Macmillan).

Until quite recently our attitude toward the atomic elements was identical with our former attitude toward fixed species. Oxygen, hydrogen, nitrogen had been there from the beginning and would always continue to be there. Whatever might be said of the organic world, the inorganic world was supposed to be a world of fixed types.

However, the discovery of radio-activity has changed this view, for it has shown us that the atom is not completely indivisible and changeless, but can break up and modify its elemental nature. The story is now a commonplace, so we need simply recall the fact that in some of the heavier elements—uranium, thorium, radium —there is a spontaneous activity which goes on transforming these elements into other elements. Thus three helium atoms are spontaneously expelled from uranium, and uranium becomes converted through thorium into radium. The expulsion of another helium atom changes radium into radium emanation. When eight helium atoms have been expelled, lead is formed.

For the most part, the other elements do not exhibit this change of their elemental forms, but the fact that we observe such changes as the above actually taking place in nature makes it impossible any longer to hold the older view that the chemical elements are fixed types. Doubtless as they stand today, for some reason not yet explained, they have a fixity of type not found in the more plastic organic world. But there is every reason to believe that change from form to form has gone on—as it still goes on—in the world of chemical orders as surely as it does in the world of organic orders. Indeed it is not inconceivable that the next great epoch-making work in science will be a work on the *Origin of Atomic Species.*

Lessening the Gap

What does all this mean for our conception of the universe? It disposes, in the first place, of the assumption that the universe is, in its fundamentals, a non-living thing. That which had appeared to be most non-living is now seen to be at least activity. More than that, it is seen to be a type of activity which exhibits two of the outstanding characteristics of life—self-maintenance and structural configuration.

"Once the new point of view is thoroughly realized and assimilated into popular thought, the bugbear of matter will cease to trouble our peace. We shall no longer continue to stare at a hopeless irreconcilable contradiction in experience. With the dissolution of the old traditional concept of matter, the dead-weight of its utter passivity will disappear from men's minds, and one of the greatest partition walls in knowledge will fall down. The contact (of matter) with life may still be very difficult to establish. But at any rate the impassable gulf will have disappeared. With the contours of matter razed, its field will itself point the way to the kingdom of life beyond. For the fields of matter and life will overlap, intermingle, and interpenetrate each other, the fruitful contacts will be established, and the enriched and broad-

ened concepts of matter and life will appear as they are
—different phases in the evolution of an essential unity.
The breakdown of the old concept of matter will have
prepared the way for a great advance toward the new
synthetic world-conception." [2]

[2] *Ibid.*, p. 52.

Chapter IV

THE DRAMA OF BIOLOGY

THE PUZZLE OF THE NEW

THE nineteenth century witnessed another significant happening—the disappearance of the soul. It was in the rapidly developing science of biology that this first occurred. Later, announcement was made by a number of workers in the field of psychology that the soul had vanished from consideration. We shall, in this chapter, disregard the psychological pronouncement and confine ourselves to what happened in biology. During the latter half of the century, most of the biologists, following the lead of the physicists, came to deal with man altogether as a physico-chemical machine.

It was doubtless well that the soul vanished from biology. It was, for all scientific purposes, a mere inscrutability. By its very nature it was subject to neither observation nor experiment. Invisible and intangible, anything could be said about it by anyone who pleased. As "vital principle," or "vital force," or "anima," or "organizing principle," or "entelechy," or "psychoid," it was the happy hunting ground for speculations that could never be checked in the laboratory. But what was yet more serious, it placed limits to experimentation. However far the scientist might go in his exploration of life, there was inevitably a point beyond which he might not go. The "soul" was forever beyond his knowing. Hence life, in the end, was fated to remain for him a mystery.

The scientist has a gently persistent way of refusing to be awed by holies of holies. When he is told that he must not enter a particular unenterable, he quietly proceeds to make preparations to walk in and take' possession. That, in brief, is the history of the development of the mechanistic theory of life in biology and later in psychology. The scientist walked into the holy of holies and found nothing there.

The story of the growing conviction of the machine-like character of life harks back to Descartes in the seventeenth century. "Even in the time of Descartes it was already clear that much of what occurs within the living body is susceptible of clear mechanical explanation. Thus the movements, whether voluntary or involuntary, of the limbs, etc., had been rendered intelligible by showing how, when muscles contract, the tendons attached to them act on the bone to which they are attached, thus bringing about mechanically the various voluntary and involuntary movements of the bodily parts attached to these bones. Kepler had shown how the crystalline lens of the eye, acting just like a glass lens, produces an image on the retina. Harvey had shown how the blood, driven mechanically by pressure from the heart, and guided by valves, is circulated round the body, carrying nutriment to and removing waste products from all parts. No one questions successfully the mechanical explanation applied in connection with these and various other processes occurring within the living body. It therefore seems natural enough to adopt the belief that all physiological processes are ultimately susceptible of similar mechanical or physico-chemical explanation." [1]

Descartes, to be sure, still retained the soul and firmly believed it to be the prime mover in conscious life. But although the soul ruled in its own sphere, the body, he taught, was a mechanism that could be conceived with all requisite adequacy without any specific reference to the soul.

A notable advance in mechanistic thinking was made when Boyle showed that air, by a purely chemical process of combustion, is a sustainer of life. This was further supported by the discovery of Priestley of the identity of chemical changes in respiration and in ordinary combustion, and by Lavoisier's interpretation of the process of oxidation. In the early part of the nineteenth century, through the chemical analysis of food and of the digestive fluids, even the mysterious process of digestion was given a chemical explanation.

Perhaps the most significant advance of all was made, however, by Schwann's discovery in 1839 that the body is made up of cell-units. Life, it now appeared, instead of being a mysterious process going on within a mysterious unanalyzable whole, was simply the sum of the processes going on within the minute cells. Later investigation was then directed toward proving that the

[1] J. S. Haldane, *The Sciences and Philosophy*, p. 20 (Doubleday Doran).

processes within and between these cells was one of a wholly chemical nature.

When Darwin's *Origin of Species* was published in 1859, it was believed that the most conclusive of all hypotheses had been adduced in support of the mechanistic theory of life. Life, according to that theory, was no inner process of self-direction and self-growth, but was, in the main, subject to external impacts. To be sure there was the still unexplained fact of initial variation, but on the whole, it was shown, species survived and changed by a process of natural selection. The process was mechanical in the sense that it was merely an interaction of external factors. Following Darwin, the greatest blow to a self-directing "spiritual" agency in the individual life was given by Weissman's refutation of the theory of the inheritance of acquired characters. What the individual does in his lifetime, according to Weissman, has no effect upon the progeny. The germ plasm carries on despite the individual's wishes or will or accomplishments. To be sure this hypothesis did not go unchallenged, but among biologists it came increasingly to hold the field.

A still more powerful support of mechanistic theory was given by Mendel's discovery of "unit-characters" and his experimentally verified hypothesis that life is simply different combinations of these life elements. What was most profoundly significant about Mendel's view was that it finally made a high degree of predictability possible in this hitherto largely unpredictable region of life. Also, in the unit-characters, he seemed to have found something that at last approached the clearly definable as well as the fundamental character of physical elements.

Most of the significant work in biology since then has followed along the line of investigation of the minute elements of life. As this investigation has continued, the picture of human life as completely determined at birth by the discrete elements in its germinal units has become the prevailing one. We are now accustomed to speak of chromosomes and genes, and we think of such physico-chemical elements—not of some mysterious "soul"—as the determinants of life. Biology, in short, seems at last to have extricated itself from the confused and fantastic vitalisms of earlier speculation, and appears to be in a fair way toward achieving that clarity, measurability, and predictability which the physicists achieved in their hypothesis of the atomic constitution of matter.

The Importance of Predictability

All this is of the profoundest significance. We may shudder somewhat at the loss of the long familiar soul, but the gain in predictability and in the control and direction of life have doubtless been no mean compensation.

For whatever problems remain over in this reduction of life to a machine—and we shall note them presently —predictability is an absolute essential if biology is to carry on its scientific work with any degree of success. Throughout all the previous centuries, life had been the paramount perplexity. We could do something with sticks and stones because we knew what we could expect of them. We could even do something with reference to the distant planets and stars. Their movements were predictable, and we could schedule our own life to a nicety years and even centuries in advance, knowing that in the heavens there is neither variableness nor shadow of change. It was different with life. The process of re-production, for example, was a mysterious event ap-parently beyond our control. We had simply to wait and see what would issue forth out of the union of lives. We might wish to produce a finer grade of offspring—as we might wish to make better bows and arrows—but there seemed no way in which we could take a controlling hand in the process. Life went on in its mysterious way and produced what it produced. Also perplexing things hap-pened to us in life, like disease and death. These, too, seemed to come out of a mystery we could only slightly control.

All through the centuries, then, life challenged us. The biology of the nineteenth century was the first really successful attempt to answer the challenge. The signif-icant point is that its success followed in the main from its frank acceptance of the fact that the only way to con-quer the mystery of life is to find the measurable and calculable elements of life, in short, to do with living beings what the physicists and chemists had done with matter. It was for this reason that the biologist had of necessity to rid himself of whatever was unanalyzable, unmeasurable, and unpredictable. For the alternatives confronted him: either the soul was to be retained, and he would then be compelled to declare life a mystery beyond understanding and control; or, the soul was to be cast out from consideration, and he was to be permitted to go ahead analyzing the life-processes until haply he should discover, with utter precision, what the determinants of those processes actually were.

Any unprejudiced review of the achievements of biology, one suspects, must justify the biologist in accepting the latter alternative. He had to be granted the right to go ahead without the obstruction of the supernatural. He had to be permitted to believe that physical life is a process subject to complete analysis.

The Puzzle of Predictability

And yet as the biologist went ahead in this more fruitful way, difficulties disclosed themselves. He felt, as we have seen, that he must achieve predictability. But how much predictability? The physicist had built for himself the ideal of a complete predictability. Analyzing the physical world into its atomic elements and formulating the laws of atomic movements, he had triumphantly concluded that, could anyone at any moment have a total knowledge of the physical configuration then present, he could know all the future course of physical events. In brief, the physicist concluded, nothing really new comes into the world. All that is to be is already determined. Novelty *appears* to enter merely because we are as yet too ignorant to know all the determining factors. But presumably the determining factors are there and have always been there. Hence, one must assume—on pain of otherwise destroying the scheme of physical uniformity—that the physical world even now is as it is to be, and nothing in heaven or on earth can change that fully determined course of events.

This might seem to be a triumph of thinking when confined to the physical world. When applied to the world of life and thought, it seems, on the other hand, to be quite the opposite. For as one easily realizes, it reduces conscious, purposive life to a nullity. We, then, only *appear* to initiate events. As a matter of fact, we initiate nothing. All that we do or are ever to do has been determined from the beginning.

Here, then, was the dilemma: either unpredictability and no control of life; or complete predictability and nothing really living to control.

A Third Alternative

There has been much worried thinking over these two alternatives. For a long time they seemed to be the only ones. Faced with the choice, and seeing no other way out, the biologist, for the most part, chose the second of the two possibilities. Better, he seemed to think, predictability and nullity therewith, than unpredictability and a mess of uncontrollable confusion.

But in recent years another alternative has been suggested, one which would seem to provide, on the one hand, for a due amount of predictability, and yet, on the other, for those qualities of initiative and novelty which seem to be most characteristic of life and particularly of conscious life.

The third alternative is called emergent evolution.[2] Its basic idea is fairly simple, but, if accepted, it at a stroke solves the gravest of the difficulties that biologists have hitherto confronted. The basic idea is that in new combinations there is something more than the additive result, or the mere sum. There is likewise an emergent new quality, which is supervenient upon the parts that have been brought together.

Let us illustrate. Hydrogen and oxygen brought together in the correct proportions eventuate in a fluid called water. Water, however, is not simply the sum of hydrogen and oxygen. It is something qualitatively new, something that cannot be found by the most searching examination of the gas, hydrogen, nor of the gas, oxygen. No amount of previous knowledge of the atomic structure of hydrogen and oxygen could, apparently, give a knowledge of this peculiar fluid that results from combining the two gases. While the quantitative result could have been predicted, namely, the sum of two atoms of hydrogen and one atom of oxygen, equalling, now, three atoms, the *qualitative* result could not have been predicted. So, likewise, when we add one more element, carbon, other new unpredictable qualities emerge. If hydrogen, oxygen, and carbon are combined in one way we get ether, if in another way, ethyl alcohol. We can pre-

---

[2] See C. L. Morgan, *Emergent Evolution.*

dict perfectly the quantitative sum of the combination, but we are powerless to predict the qualitative results.

Thus in every new combination there is a new emergent quality. We find this fact multiplied a millionfold throughout nature. Molecules combine, and we have hitherto unknown emergent qualities. Chemistry is a brilliant enterprise of inventing qualitatively new substances. So, in like manner, is the hybridizing art. We unite a horse and an ass. Now that the mule has come, we indeed go on expecting muleness as a result of the combination. Before the first uniting it would have been impossible to predict the precise qualities that eventuated in the mule. The same is true of the cross-breeding of plants. Qualities appear that are in many cases exceedingly different from those of the original strain. As a matter of fact, "the inability to predict results from a knowledge of the properties of the parents used has always been a fascinating feature of hybridism." [3]

Indeed, this writer goes on to say, "It might be challenged if there is any object or substance, beyond the protons and electrons, non-living or living, from atom to galaxy, which is not actually an advent of the emergent new."

Saving Predictability

Emergent evolution, then, saves novelty. Always and everywhere the new is coming into being. What does it do to predictability? It should not be difficult to see that

[3] Robert K. Nabours, *A Third Alternative: Emergent Evolution*, (Scientific Monthly, Nov., 1930, p. 445).

it saves just the predictability that is necessary, and no more. Thus, to illustrate, we now can easily predict that when we combine H_2 and O, we shall have water. We need have no reasonable doubts about the matter. Before we made the combination of the two gases, we could not predict. Water was a new emergent. But now that we know what happens, we can make the same combination millions of times and expect the same results. The same is true of animal-, and of plant-hybridizing.

In brief, we have here all the predictability that is necessary for a powerful control of both the non-living and living factors of our experience. We can go ahead, then, searching for new discoveries. As soon as we make them, we can repeat the processes and obtain the same results.

We have all the predictability that is necessary, but not too much. Too much predictability, as we have seen, simply nullifies the whole procedure. For it rules out initiative. Obviously initiative can have meaning only as there is the possibility of the bringing of something novel into existence.

Thus the hypothesis of emergent evolution seems to achieve both the ends that we most highly desire: it enables us to go forward in the predictable control of life, and it enables us also to believe that we are actually going forward and not eternally standing still.

New Independence for Biology

Professor Jennings has hailed the doctrine of emergent evolution as "the declaration of independence of biology." It is not difficult to understand why. As long as biology was headed for a complete predictability, it was necessary to believe that "the only method of learning about the organic is to study the inorganic." In short, biology was forced to become physics. Every living creature had to be studied *not in terms of its own unique configuration* but in terms of its constituent physico-chemical parts.

"What difference," asks Professor Jennings,[4] "does it make if we accept the doctrine of emergent evolution, rather than that of mechanical evolution?" "It makes a very great difference," he answers. "For mechanical evolution the ideal scientific method is mainly rationalistic, to but a minimal extent empirical. From the examination of any small part of the universe, at any time, it is possible to discover the laws of action, of grouping, for all its parts and for all periods. Only a few preliminary observations should be required—of the particles, their arrangements and motions. The rest is a matter of computing, of reasoning. Science should quickly leave its toe-touch with observation and soar away in mathematical calculations, in philosophical reasonings. From a sample of the universe we ought to be able to reason out the rest. Continued recourse to experimentation is but a device of feeble minds; an attempt to discover in a rude manner what we should know by calculations and logic.

"For the doctrine of emergent evolution, on the other

[4] H. S. Jennings, *The Biological Basis of Human Nature*, p. 371 (W. W. Norton & Company, Inc.).

hand, observation and experiment are the primary and the final methods of science, never to be laid aside. They are *the* methods for learning of the universe. . . .

"The doctrine of emergent evolution makes a great difference to one's conception of the relations between the living and the non-living . . . It repudiates the notion that the best interpreter of the living is he who confines himself to the study of the non-living; a notion that has been the curse of biological science, condemning it to move in pretentious superficialities. . . . When this is recognized the practice of facile generalization which honeycombs biological science with error will lose its seductive charm. . . . Divergent results of experimentation in different organisms are not to be rejected on *a priori* grounds; diversities are as significant as uniformities. This state of affairs, which on the one hand is a corollary of emergent evolution, is revealed on the other hand by the advance of experimental biology; things living behave as if emergent evolution were a true doctrine."

Thus the doctrine of emergent evolution seems at last to have extricated us from a most difficult dilemma. We need no longer believe that in order to preserve predictability we must confine our attention to the atomic elements; we can believe in the continuous emergence of new qualities in the world; we can experimentally work with those new emergents; we can furthermore believe that the later in evolution has an even greater significance than the earlier. And so at last we can turn our backward-looking faces forward and go ahead with the confident conviction that there are new things under the sun and that we ourselves can play no inconsiderable part in bringing them into being.

Part Two

MAN A REVEALER

Through the porthole I can see
One tiny circle of blue, cloud-flecked—
Because it is there
I know there is also
The infinite sky—remote, mysteriously sure.

BONARO WILKINSON

Chapter V

EVOLUTION ON THE HUMAN LEVEL

TOWARD MORE WIDELY FUNCTIONING WHOLES

EVOLUTION means many things to many persons. It is by no means an unambiguous idea. And yet it is the key-idea of our modern civilization.

What does evolution really mean? There is the biologist's meaning, which is usually not the meaning held by the common man. The strict biologist means by evolution simply change of species. Whether that change is for the better or the worse is to him irrelevant. The important thing for him is that species change into other species. There is also the geologist's view, which regards the slow transformation of the earth's rock configurations. There is no thought in his mind that in this transformation rocks are getting better and better. There is finally the astronomer's point of view. He notes the change of celestial forms—from nebulous masses, let us say, into stars and planetary systems, and on again, perhaps, to nebulous masses. Whether the whole process is getting somewhere does not concern him.

For the common man, on the other hand, evolution almost invariably means progress. More especially, it means progress from lower life to higher life, the whole culminating in man. Just why man should have the

67

honor of being the culminating point of evolution he is doubtless never quite sure, but he takes it for granted that the whole evolutional process has tended toward man. Also, why there should have been—and still are—many offshoots not leading toward man, he likewise does not know. For the most part, he does not give the matter a thought, or if he does, he is content to say, with confident optimism, that nature is a great experimenter and can afford to try out many different ways of getting things accomplished. The important point, as he sees it, is that an erect creature has at last been achieved.

There are also other ambiguities in the use of the term evolution. For many persons, evolution is synonymous with something grim and bloody. They have been impressed by a single phrase, the struggle for survival, and they have pictured the universe, and mankind as well, as engaged in a long continued conflict.

If they are one kind of person they deplore this. They ask, sadly, how love can be supreme in such a universe. They were taught that the universe, in the person of its creator, is love. But love does not fight. Love suffers, understands, is kind. If evolution, they say, is this slaughter in order to survive, then evolution is a travesty of the good life.

They may, however, be another kind of person. Then they embrace evolution eagerly and find in it good reason for their most cherished and self-gratifying behavior. Evolution, to them, is a justification of the competitive way of life. To grow strong, to fight hard, to put the foe out of the running—that is nature's way, and that must be man's way. Not softness; hardness. Not giving; taking. Not compassion; power. Strong armies, strong nations, strong businesses. Nature's way—and man's way.

Again, there are others who deny all this. They have read beyond the phrase, "struggle for survival." They may have read Kropotkin's *Mutual Aid* and become impressed with the large amount of coöperation—symbiosis—within the universe. Nature, to them, is not simply red in tooth and claw, and man, therefore, is not simply justified in ruthless destruction of his competitors. Life advances best, they believe, as it gives mutual aid. They deplore the attitude of those who, from too hasty observation, believe that evolution rules love out of the universe. If love means mutuality, they say, then evolution, as in large measure a symbiotic or coöperative process, is nature's great way of love.

Difficulty of Understanding Subhuman Orders

Where shall one find clarity amidst such conflicting views? It is important to note that the views customarily held of evolution are invariably based upon biological and physical data. But presumably there is evolution also on the human level. This, however, is not the kind of evolution that is usually conceived when the term is used either scientifically or popularly. Evolution for the most part suggests ichthyosauri, swordfish, panthers. It suggests the fight of the wolf-pack for food, the leap of the tiger and the swift dart of the bird. Or it suggests the slow emergence of planetary systems out of star dust.

It would be folly to minimize the importance of the scientists' researches and of their consequent views of evolution. They have succeeded in changing our conceptions of the world so notably that the old, static, heaven-appointed order has happily disappeared. And yet it is significant to realize that they are dealing with orders of existence with which they themselves as human creatures have only the most external connection. Thus the biologist, for example, cannot hold illuminating converse with the amœba which he is watching or the guinea pig which he is subjecting to experiment. He may indeed be able to observe from the outside; but he does not know—and perhaps can never know—what is going on inside these creatures. He is dealing, in short, with that which, in the very nature of things, he is barred from fully understanding. Also—and this is of considerable importance—he is dealing with orders of existence that presumably are low in the scale of development. If, among his animal orders, he discovers certain processes going on, it may be that these are by no means the most significant processes in the universe, for the simple reason that other, more significant processes are yet to develop or have already developed in higher orders of being. The astronomer is in even greater difficulty. He views his star substance through a telescope. He gets a report of it through millions of light-years of space. When the geologist brings some of it closely under his eyes—as physical matter on this earth—he is never able to put himself inside the matter which he examines. Like the biologist and the astronomer, he, too, is restricted to an outside view. He can therefore only observe as a spectator observes and report as an external spectator may. Herein, perhaps, lies the profoundest difficulty which we encounter in our efforts to understand the significance of evolution. We have grown accustomed to thinking of evolution solely on the level of the biologist, the geologist, and the astronomer, not realizing that on those levels it is not only impossible to understand fully what is taking place, but that what actually is taking place may be only a most elementary part of the story.

Where We Get Behind the Scenes

Without in any sense detracting from the great achievements of the three sciences mentioned, our thinking might be turned in a fruitful direction if we should start in quite a different way. Let us start on that level of life where we are capable of being, so to speak, on the inside. In a sense—doubtless a very restricted one—you, the reader, know yourself from the inside. And so do I. Neither you nor I can know paramecia or earthworms with quite the intimacy of understanding with which we know ourselves. This, of course, is not saying a great deal, for our ignorance of ourselves is doubtless profound. But it is saying something. Also, because you and I are much akin, you can have a fair guess as to what is taking place in me, as I, likewise, can have a fair guess at what is taking place in you. In other words, it would seem reasonable to start where our information is the most intimate and first hand.

Let us examine our human life in its most typical processes. There is first the process of growing from infancy to maturity. We know that what happened in our life is something like this. We came into the world as helpless infants unable as yet to control parts of ourselves and our world. We could not hold a spoon and convey food to our mouths. We could not walk nor talk. But we grew up. What, now, did growing up mean? It meant a process of bringing increasing areas of ourselves —our muscles, sense organs—and increasing areas of our world within our control. It was a process, in short, of becoming more widely functioning wholes.

That is the typical process in the life of the individual —becoming a more widely functioning whole. The process goes on in all kinds of ways. The child learns to manipulate not only his fingers but also toys and tools. In other words, he learns how to incorporate these apparently foreign substances into the fabric of his life. Later he begins to own things, things as dissimilar both to himself and to one another as clothes, trunks, golf clubs, houses, automobiles, yachts. Here again we note the incorporation of wider areas of the environment into his functioning life. But he also takes in other parts of his environment—ideas, scientific laws, poetic emotions, ethical obligations.

To become a really mature individual, he must have passed far beyond the restricted area of childhood functioning and have established himself as a functioning whole capable of maintaining himself through the integration within himself of a fairly large amount of physical and mental reality.

The process, as we know, does not go on with equal success in the case of all individuals. Some remain pretty much on the childhood level. Some—like idiots—remain even below the level of normal childhood. Some advance to an average adulthood—that is, they achieve sufficiently wide integration to get along fairly well. Others—like the Pasteurs and the Shakespeares—advance to superior adulthood. The characteristic of the last is that they hold many more aspects of reality in an illuminating unity of life than do most individuals.

Evolution on the Human Level

Let us turn now to what we call evolution on the human level. We speak, for example, of the evolution of law and justice. We speak also of the evolution of the family, the state, art, education, religion, business organization, manners, morals. In every case we take it for granted that we are considering not merely changes which take place from one condition to another, but changes toward what is more adequate.

What, in such evolution, do we mean by "more adequate"? Let us take an example from law and justice. In primitive days there was the eye-for-an-eye stage. Why do we consider that far less adequate than even the inadequate processes that prevail today? Obviously, the eye-for-an-eye type of justice left certain essential matters out of consideration. For example, it made no effort to find out whether the injury inflicted was accidental or intended. Modern justice, on the other hand, takes such a fundamental matter into consideration. Thus modern justice to that extent functions in terms of a wider area of relationships. It incorporates into its processes something that the older forms left out.

The same is true of the evolution of the family. We do not hesitate to say that the cave-man stage, where primitive man took possession of his mate simply as so much chattel, was a low stage of family life, because at that stage the male functioned in terms of a narrow range of experience. We have no hesitation in believing that a type of life in which the man woos the woman, wins her, is tender to her, builds a home and family with her, yields her a large freedom for the development of her own life, is a far more adequate form of sexual union. Again, the reason is simple. The male, in this case, functions in terms of a wider conception of the relationships. He is aware of feelings in his mate of which his primitive ancestor was quite unconscious. He is also aware of other possibilities in the union. Thus the later family is an improvement upon the primitive one because it is a functioning unity which operates in terms of more of what there actually is in the situation.

We could pursue the matter into various other regions of human life, considering the evolution of religion, politics, art, scientific method, poetry, the novel, the rights of women. In every case we should find that where evolution means a progress it signifies what we have just indicated, a wider functioning.

Evolution, then, on the human level, is a movement from a type of functioning which excludes significant factors to types of functioning that progressively integrate more of these factors.

Man as a Child of Nature

We seem here to reach an important conclusion. There is a prevalent tendency among those of us who have emancipated ourselves from the naïve religious views of our ancestors and have accepted the more rigorously critical views of the scientist to assert that nature, as it is now described, is wholly without purpose, meaning, or direction. In physical terms, it is atoms combining and recombining, with no purpose and no goal. In biological terms, it is a constant change of life forms, a change, however, that has neither direction nor end in view. Nature, supposedly, has neither purpose nor meaning. But this, obviously, cannot be completely true, for we note that on the human level nature exhibits a purposeful, meaningful, and directional type of process. The human creature, as we have seen, moves in the direction of more adequate functioning. To that end he integrates more of the situation into his activities and so achieves for himself and his kind a more widely sustaining whole of life.

This, however, may sound like a strange way of expressing things. Man, we are usually led to believe, is not nature, and therefore what may be true of man is not to be taken as in any sense true of nature. Nature, in short, is supposed to be everything that is other than man. Sometimes we are made to think that man fights nature. For example he builds up ethical codes which he does not find in nature. Nature is grim, bloody. Man, so we are told, tries to overcome nature and builds a life of mutual give and take that succeeds despite nature's difficult processes. Sometimes, again, we are made to think that nature fights man. There are tornadoes, thunder and lightning, earthquakes, invading hosts of insects, sudden climatic changes. Thus man, we are taught, is a creature apart. He belongs to another order.

But this, when one thinks about it critically, can surely not be true. Is it not a left-over of the old dualism that produced, among other things, the religion of supernatural magic? There were supposed to be two spheres —the natural and the supernatural—and man was supposed to belong by kinship to the supernatural.

All our later thinking, however, tends to go counter to this. The trend of modern science has been in the direction of making man a creature of nature. If, then, we find certain qualities in man, we must apparently conclude that they are qualities which, to that extent, belong to nature. Man, in short, is nature on one of nature's levels.

Man, therefore, does not fight nature. On the contrary, what we call "fighting nature" is merely man's refusal to remain within the narrow areas in which he first finds himself. He struggles to release himself into wider areas. His ethical codes, for example, mark the development of more adequate ways of functioning. Thus he fights his limited nature, not Nature.

In point of fact, creatures which we ordinarily regard as so intimately parts of nature that we always think of them when we use the word "nature" are largely isolated from wide relationship with nature. They move within exceedingly limited fields. They have only the smallest contact with the nature around them. Man, on the other hand, has the power to make contact with nature far more widely. When, for example, he discovers the movements of the planets, the laws of chemical combination, the sequences of the seasons, the principles of organic growth and decay, it is not an exaggeration to say that he is far more intimately and understandingly a child of nature than the armadillo that noses about ignorant of all these matters.

It seems that we need to impress upon ourselves this rather novel idea, for the reverse one has too long held sway. *Man is far more a child of nature than any of the animals or plants around him.* And he is increasingly a child of nature as the growth of his intelligence makes him able to make contact with nature more widely.

But if this is true, then a profoundly important further fact is true. What man exhibits in himself—of qualities and processes—belongs to nature, indeed, *is* nature on the level of humanity. When we regard matters in this light, it is seen that man exhibits in himself far more of what nature is and can be than do any of the animals or plants around him.

We have so accustomed ourselves to thinking of nature in animal-terms and plant-terms—and, more recently, in atom-terms—that to think of it in terms of that which we find on the human level seems illegitimate. It goes counter to everything that we have latterly considered scientific. And yet the foregoing considerations would seem to hold. Man, with his wider understanding and mastery, does actually reveal more of nature than do the more limited creatures. May we not say, then, that our traditional habit of looking to animal and plant and atom for exclusive illumination about the universe has, in large measure, been a self-defeating one? [1]

Suppose, now, that we should change this curiously self-defeating habit of ours. While, indeed, we should continue our researches in the regions of physical and biological nature, would we not turn a keen eye to nature as it functions on its apparently most illuminating level?

Since the birth of modern science, that has practically never been done. The psychological and ethical processes have indeed been studied, but only in and for themselves, not as clues to the interpretation of reality. The time is apparently now ripe for a penetrating research into the human processes, a research to be carried on with the confident expectation that as we learn about

[1] We have an example of this self-defeating kind of thinking in Mr. Joseph Wood Krutch's sentence: "Living is a physiological phenomenon with only a physiological meaning." That statement being an evaluation, it is itself more than physiological. See *The Modern Temper* (Harcourt, Brace & Company) for an extended instance of such fallacious thinking.

these processes we shall discover many things that are deeply significant about the larger universe.

Error of Anthropomorphism

What hinders us from doing this is a shuddering remembrance of man's naïve anthropomorphism. We must never again commit those childish follies of translating the great forces of reality into human forms. We must not crowd the hills and valleys with spirits, make the moon into a pallid female, or the sun into a god of flaming beauty. We must not have deities descending unexpectedly out of the heavens, changing the course of things. We must have no Jehovah walking in the garden, or delivering tablets of stone on a mountain top.

But perhaps we have leaned too far backwards. Perhaps there was a kind of childish wisdom in these imaginings. It may even be that it was in some respects a better wisdom than the later sophistication which translated the grandeur and mystery and everlasting vitality of nature into bumping atoms and struggling brutes.

For what this childish imagining did realize, despite the exceedingly naïve forms in which it expressed itself, was the essential kinship between man, the thinking, purposing, creating being, and his world. The world, to that childish imagining, was not a grotesquely or terrifyingly alien thing. It had a kind of friendliness about it —the friendliness of powers that could relate themselves to man's own life. And even if some of these powers were ominous, they could be appealed to, perhaps assuaged.

We are ready now to put away the childish parts of this belief. Nymphs and satyrs, spirits, demons, gods and goddesses do not belong to our modern world. But if they are cast out, must they leave an utter void? Must we decide that the whole thing was a stupid falsity and look blankly, if triumphantly, at an unfriendly universe of meaningless physical movements?

The mistake that our anthropomorphic ancestors made is easily understandable. It lay in taking the more obvious but irrelevant qualities in man and making them into the picture of the governing forces of the universe. They did not, in short, penetrate to the enduring essentials of human nature. It was for this reason that they could build their naïve conception of an Olympus with its pleasure-hunting, carefree, jealous, wrangling, deceitful, and more or less irresponsible gods and goddesses. It was for this reason that they could imagine the universe in the person of a fierce, opinionated, self-glorifying, doting Jehovah. To be sure, they built in terms of human qualities, but of qualities that were all too narrowly and too transiently human.

When we suggest, now, that human nature reveals more fully than any order of life what reality is and has it in it to be, we mean by human nature, human nature in its more enduring essentials.

Individuals are, indeed, jealous, angry, selfish, ignorant, cruel. Since these qualities are human, they, too, belong to nature. But they seem not to be of lasting stuff. Nature, on the human level, seems gradually to be getting rid of them or at least to be diminishing their life-defeating power. What are the persistent essentials of human nature? That now becomes our problem.

Thus far we have caught a glimpse of one quality or process which seems fundamental and persistent in human life. It is the process of integrating more of reality into one's functioning self, of becoming, in short, a more widely adequate whole.

It is in this drive toward more widely functioning life that something deeply essential in nature seems to be revealed. If human beings have this drive, then nature, the source and continuer of us, must *to that extent* be credited with the same drive. But then nature is apparently not meaningless nor directionless. In one aspect of its being, at least, it is a progressive achievement of increasingly significant wholes.

Evolution on Subhuman Levels

All this seems clear on the human level. Can anything be said of plant, animal, and atom?

There is, as we pointed out in the preceding chapter, a tendency at present to think in terms of emergent evolution. The organic, it is believed, has emerged from the inorganic, the psychic from the organic. When we think in these terms we imply that the emergent is somehow more adequate than that out of which it has emerged. Is there any ground for this belief?

It seems obvious that the parts or elements of inorganic nature—oxygen, hydrogen, nitrogen, etc.,—are more stereotyped in their forms, more repetitive in their processes than the parts or members of organic nature. The organic emerged, apparently, when elements were evolved—like carbon—which were less rigidly stable. They could make more varied contacts. The more stable atoms were like relatively impermeable units, set in their ways. They could maintain only the most narrowly restricted order of relationships, could combine only along a few well grooved lines.

When the protoplasmic atom—the cell—was evolved, apparently a surprisingly new flexibility was achieved. The cell not only had within itself the most complex atomic structure, but it had the power to make contact with its environing world in more complicated and changing ways. It could grow by progressively complicated inner differentiation and by accretion. We would seem justified in surmising, then, that the evolution of the organic out of the inorganic meant the development of functioning wholes that were able to make contact with wider areas of reality.

The same idea carries on into the evolution of the psychological out of the merely organic. The life-process of a Darwin or a Goethe, or even of an average human being, is so far more widely and powerfully integrated than that of the simple amœba that there is really no comparison between the two.

All of nature, then—if we accept the emergent view —exhibits a process or drive toward more widely functioning wholes. What we find on the human level, in short, is then not something alien and apart. It is something that runs true to nature's form. Human nature

differs from other forms of nature simply in the greater
powers through which it has released itself from too narrow areas of functioning.

Nature Articulate in Man

This conception is finely expressed in a poem written
in the contemporary spirit. I doubt whether one would
find anything quite like it in the older poetry, for the
older poetry sprang out of a different—in the main a
dualistic—conception of nature and man. At least there
was in the older poetry no conception of the slow development of nature itself and therefore no thought of
finding in man the clearest revelation of what nature is
and can be. But this contemporary poet, unperturbed by
mysteries of atoms or protoplasmic elementals, goes
straight to the issue:

> "If you would know what earth is, scan
> The intricate, proud heart of man,
> Which is the earth articulate,
> And learn how holy and how great,
> How limitless and how profound
> Is the nature of the ground. . . .

> "For she is pity, she is love,
> All wisdom she, all thoughts that move
> About her everlasting breast
> Till she gathers them to rest:
> All tenderness of all the ages,

Seraphic secrets of the sages, . . .
All prayer, all anguish, and all tears
Are but the dust, that from her dream
Awakes, and knows herself supreme—
Are but earth when she reveals
All that her secret heart conceals
Down in the dark and silent loam,
Which is ourselves asleep, at home.
Yea, and this my poem, too,
Is part of her as dust and dew,
Wherein herself she doth declare
Through my lips, and say her prayer. . . .

"Deftly does the dust express
In mind her hidden loveliness,
And from her cool silence stream
The cricket's cry and Dante's dream:
For the earth that breeds the trees
Breeds cities, too, and symphonies,
Equally her beauty grows
Into a savior, or a rose." [2]

A view like this is significant because it gives us a new mode of approach to the perplexing problem of life and the universe. If man, in some measure, reveals nature, then the search after the great essentials in man's life will, to a degree, reveal something of the cosmic essentials. It would seem, then, to be a curious inversion to go seeking exclusively among the atoms and the lower

[2] John Hall Wheelock, *Earth* (The Yale Review). The order of the lines has been slightly changed.

orders of organic nature when we have at our hand a type of life in which nature apparently functions in a peculiarly significant way.

Thus a method of approach is open to us which would seem to be valuable for two reasons. As we search out the great essentials of human life, we learn the better to understand our own life. If, however, in the understanding of that life we further gain some degree of understanding of the universe in which we live, we would seem to have achieved double measure.

The method is at least worth trying. The nineteenth century, concentrating on the machine-like processes of matter and the sanguinary processes of the lower orders of animal life, left us with a universe that was fairly dismal. Now this may actually be the only kind of universe there is. If so, we shall have to rest content with it. But the twentieth century, as we have seen, has already repudiated the apparent finalities of those views. May it not be possible, as we confidently advance from the study of atoms and protoplasmic cells to the study of man, that some new illumination will come which will change the universe from meaninglessness into meaning, and thereby the life and destiny of man from a kind of futility into some measure of significance?

Chapter VI

MAN GOES HIS NEW WAY

THE HUMAN PROCESS OF ADVOLUTION

WE enter, then, upon our search for the great essentials of human life. The presumption, as we carry on the search, will be that wherever we find something that is enduringly significant among ourselves, we shall likewise have found something that has significance in the larger universe. We are deliberately, in short, attempting to see nature as far as we can through man. We say this plainly and emphatically, knowing well the criticisms to which we at once subject ourselves. We shall be accused of a return to anthropomorphism. But historic anthropomorphism, as we have pointed out, failed, not because it tried to find in man realities that reveal truths about the universe, but because it knew too little about the real nature of man. There was, however, another and more important reason for the failure of historic anthropomorphism. It pictured reality as actually *human* in form. In other words, it imagined its Zeuses, Heras, Jehovahs and the rest to be creatures very like human beings. That was a childishly uncritical procedure and one which we have now fairly outlived.

In the pages that follow we shall be emphasizing not that man is the pattern upon whom we must build our conception of the universe—making God, as the saying is, in the image of ourselves—but rather that man has qualities in him that reveal significant facts about the universe. In short, we prefer to look to man rather than solely to the atom for our chief source of illumination.

In the last chapter, by being willing to consider what happens on the human level, we seemed to discover one basic fact about human life, namely, that it is, both in its individual and its collective processes, a movement toward the formation of more widely functioning wholes. With this as a clue, it seems not impossible that some such movement is to be found in other regions of the universe—in the processes of animal life and particularly in the processes whereby organic life emerges out of inorganic matter. But we should reserve judgment on this. These orders of existence are still too far removed from our intimate knowledge for us to say much about them. Nevertheless, if the clue should turn out to be a true one, we would seem justified in believing the universe to be not a meaningless and directionless affair, but a manifold process that operates by realizing within itself significant wholes.

Let us leave these wider and more difficult matters, however, and return to the examination of human existence.

Classing Us with the Subhuman

There is one profoundly significant type of activity that takes place on the human level. We really need a name for it, and unfortunately we have none. Thus far the word "evolution" has been used indiscriminately to indicate what happens when animal orders change and when man achieves new ways of life. Thus we speak, without essential distinction, of the evolution of crustacea and the evolution of art.

Doubtless there is a kind of poetic justice in this. The word "evolution" has united us all in one common destiny—ant-eaters, hyenas, rhinoceroses, monkeys, and man. If that hurts our feelings, no doubt we have deserved it. We had been perhaps a little too arrogant in our claim to a special place in the universe. Nineteenth-century biological science quite properly took down our egotism and showed us that we were, in the scale of development, only animals a little higher than the rest.

A good part of our modern psychology is an attempt to make this so clear that we shall not easily forget it. We are admonished that practically all of our behavior springs from the animal sublevels of our life. Sometimes these sublevel processes are referred to as instincts. We are warned that, highly idealistic as our behaviors may seem to be, they are all, in fact, simply expressions of a few elemental drives—chiefly for self-preservation, food, and sex. Indeed, we are being told this so frequently and so earnestly that we begin to feel that a really sophisticated individual will have no idealistic illusions. He will be frankly and courageously an animal.

Evolution Emphasizes the Past

The difficulty, it would seem, lies in a failing that is not infrequent. We have taken a single word to cover a multitude of distinctions. Evolution is a notable word that has carried our thought forward in so fruitful a manner that we have come to regard it with what approaches finality. If we are not careful, however, this may be not a little disastrous to our clear thinking. It may be that the common idea of evolution does not tell the whole story; indeed that the word itself demands the telling of more of it.

The emphasis in the word evolution is, commonly, upon a past—a past *out of which* we have come. Etymologically the word means a "rolling out of." Our preoccupation in the study of evolution has had of necessity to be with earlier forms and with the processes by which later forms emerged from them. In that study, practically no thought has been given to the future nor to the direction in which we are going. The obvious reason, of course, has been that we know nothing of the future nor of direction toward the future. Unless we would involve ourselves in fruitless speculation, therefore, it has seemed best to hold ourselves to what we know. We know that we come from lowlier past forms.

This would not be so unfortunate if it did not lead us to make certain misleading assumptions about life. Impressed with this image of the human forms rolling, so to speak, out of subhuman forms, we tend to look exclusively for information and for guidance to this ancestral element in us.

But suppose we should turn to what is most characteristic about human behavior. It is obvious that all human behavior springs out of needs. These needs, however, are of two kinds. One kind unites us to the lower forms of life; the other indicates that we have emerged to another level on which we are sharply distinguished from the lower forms and are enabled to act in ways that are characteristically and indeed powerfully different.

Compulsive Needs

The type of need that unites us with the lower animal forms is characterized by a certain compulsiveness. I have hunger, let us say, and I cast about as best I can to find the food that will satisfy my hunger. I am in this no different from all the living creatures, plant and animal, that inhabit the world. Or I am beaten upon by a storm and seek shelter. Again, a common kinship. Or I meet a foe and set about to defend myself. Or I have an urge to the opposite sex.

All of these needs in me are elemental and compulsory. I cannot escape responding to them. They are organic drives that are prior to all conscious plan or reasoning.

In biological language we speak of such behaviors as *tropisms*. The plant is geotropic and heliotropic. Its roots are compelled to go downward, its stalk upward. All living creatures are chemotropic. They must inevitably go toward the kinds of foods that nourish them. All sexed animals are genotropic. They must respond to certain sex stimuli.

It has been suggested that all human behavior should be described in terms of tropisms. But it may be possible to go too far in this direction. For a distinction has to be made between such compulsive needs as we have described and needs that seem to be so different in their inception and operation that they cannot properly be classed with the tropisms.

The Advolutional Level of Evolution

These latter needs, instead of being inescapably compulsive, have about them a certain quality of voluntariness. Also they admit a new element—a more or less clear previsioning of the future. I decide, let us say, to take up the study of European history. I am not compelled to that. I could refrain from doing it and still live quite happily. It cannot be said that there is in me any European-history-tropism. Note now what I do. I lay out a plan. I think ahead for a year, two years, let us say. I organize what I am to do. That *organization in terms of the future*, then, becomes a determining factor in my life. It causes me to do things of one sort and another. It is something *toward* which I consciously move. While it is, indeed, an e-volution, a rolling out of the past, it is far more predominantly an ad-volution, a turning *toward* something previsioned.

It is necessary to study this advolutional type of evolution a little more closely, for it is not only the most characteristic but also the most fruitful of the human processes. It marks man as a new achievement in nature. The animal and plant are not yet on the advolutional level, for they apparently cannot clearly prevision a future. That is why they remain for such long periods where they are. That, also, is why their evolution is at the mercy of external forces beyond their control.

With the coming of the advolutional power, however, the process of change becomes greatly accelerated: we now call it progress. Primitive man thinks out a way of crossing a turbulent stream. He projects possibilities and builds some kind of clumsy raft. Later, at a less primitive stage, he builds a bridge. Later, he sends a train of cars across the bridge. Later he spurns the ground altogether and flies across the water. It is an unfortunate leaning over backwards to minimize all this for the sake of showing how much we are like animals. In this respect we are so unlike animals that we belong within another domain. Nature, in short, in the advolutional creature—the creature that can constantly make the unreal future real—has accomplished a new triumph.

With advolution, as we have said, a new kind of causality enters. The prevailing causality on the lower levels of life is what has been called *vis a tergo*—a force or push from behind. The scientist may describe it as an antecedent to its consequent. Hunger is a *vis a tergo*. It drives us. So is the sex urge. So is the fear that sends us flying from disaster. But advolutional causality is different. It is, as it were, a pull from in front. The unrealized future is ahead of us. We set up a plan. There it is, unactualized as yet; but the plan is something toward which we move.

What is this toward which we move? In every case it is something which we conceive to be superior to that which at present exists. To be able to cross the turbulent stream is better than to remain impotently on the bank. To cross it on a bridge is better than to cross it on a clumsy raft. To send a train of cars across the bridge is better than to cross it afoot or in a slow drawn cart. To be sure, that which we conceive to be superior may not really be so. We make mistakes. We choose the less worthy, believing it to be the more worthy. But what we choose is always *to us* the superior.

The Central Human Problem

Here, then, man is unique. He can be conscious of what is superior and move toward it. It is his most significant power. Indeed the more clearly and continuously it operates in human life, the more effective, and, shall we say, happy life becomes. If we wish to know then what human nature significantly is, we must turn, not to those qualities which man has in common with plant and animal, but to this quality which is specifically his own. It is said that to be really happy one must live in harmony with one's essential nature. Hitherto we have thought of that essential nature chiefly in terms of food, fighting, and sex, the qualities that man inherits from his past. But if his essential life reaches its unique level when there is a conscious moving toward something that is conceivably superior, then we shall have to say that man is happiest in the degree that he moves in that direction.

It will be worth while to consider for a moment the bearing which the advolutional process has upon the question: what is the best or most successful way in which to live? That question has, in man's history, been answered in three major ways.

Hedonism

In the first place, it has been noted that man is a creature of pleasure and pain. It has been observed that pain, unless it serves the end of securing greater pleasure, is an evil, while pleasure, unless it leads to a greater pain, is a good. Only a very foolish person would declare that pain is good in and of itself; and only a curiously twisted nature would declare that pleasure of any kind whatever is an evil. This view seems axiomatic. The sensible business of life, therefore, would seem to be to eliminate pain as fully as possible, and as fully as possible to achieve pleasure. This is *Hedonism*.

The difficulty with this view, however, is that, as a pure pleasure-pain theory, not further qualified, it takes no explicit and discriminating account of different levels of satisfaction. One may, as we know, be quite happy on the animal level. But does one wish to be chiefly an animal? John Stuart Mill asked: "Would you rather be a pig satisfied than a Socrates dissatisfied?" The whole issue lies in the kind of choice one makes between animal and human states. If one chooses the human, one accepts the fact that man has reached a level where a kind of joyous dissatisfaction is the supreme satisfaction. On that level the chief business of living is not found in the gratification of elemental wants that more or less insistently drive us, but rather in the pursuit of the unattained. Life, in other words, on this level, is most successful when it is not yet successful.

This was what Schopenhauer, for example, could not understand. Finding life to be an endless striving, he could see only agony in the unsatisfaction of the process. But why should this unsatisfaction be agony? It will be agony only if measured by animal standards which go no further than the avoidance of pain and the achievement of animal satisfactions. But with man a new kind of happiness has entered the scheme of reality, the happiness of having a prevision of the superior and of going endlessly toward its achievement.

So the pleasure-pain theory is inadequate because it does not make clear the distinction between the animal and the human levels of satisfaction. If man is, in his supreme capacity, a creature such as we have described, then his most intense and lasting joys can come only when he acts in his uniquely human way.

Stoicism

There is a second major view that has had its place among men. It looks upon life a good deal more sternly. It sees dangers, difficulties, disappointments. It realizes that if man gives way to these, he becomes a sorry creature of anxieties, fears, and despairs. It seeks a way out by stiffening man's courage. But it can stiffen his courage only as it convinces him that there is some sense in the whole scheme of things. To ask him to endure pain when the pain is simply a monstrosity, would seem even less intelligent than the behavior of animals, who try in every way to avoid whatever pain they can.

This second view, therefore, emphasizes the fundamental rightness of things. "The Lord giveth; the Lord taketh away; blessed be the name of the Lord." "God's in his heaven, all's right with the world." "Whatever may happen to thee," said the Roman Stoic, "it was prepared for thee from all eternity." [1]

The Stoics were the master endurers. We admire such individuals for their toughness. It is a question, however, whether we should admire them greatly for their insight. We suspect that to endure ills—even with bravely set lips—is really less admirable than to endeavor—with a wrinkling of the brow—to find a way out of them.

Stoicism is noble, perhaps, but it seems less than fully intelligent. May not the unintelligence lie in the fact that this endurance theory does not accept man on his

---

[1] Marcus Aurelius, *Meditations*, Book X; 5.

essentially human level? It really accepts him on the animal level as a part of a system organized and ruled by powers greater than himself. It accepts him as a creature born, living his appointed way, dying, and returning whence he came.

There are times, to be sure, when one must have the courage to endure. But endurance is significant only as it serves a recognized end beyond itself. Prometheus, chained to the rock, endured nobly, because he was a rebel against unjust powers. There was greatness in the courage that refused to surrender. His was endurance on the advolutional level, because it was illuminated and inspired by a vision of something better.

"To suffer woes which Hope thinks infinite;
  To forgive wrongs darker than death or night;
    To defy Power, which seems omnipotent;
  To love, and bear; to hope till Hope creates
  From its own wreck the thing it contemplates;
    Neither to change, nor falter, nor repent;
  This, like thy glory, Titan, is to be
  Good, great and joyous, beautiful and free;
  This is alone Life, Joy, Empire, and Victory!" [2]

Thus Stoicism as a way of life is hardly sufficient. It minimizes man's intelligence and power to set wrong things right. It hands him over too easily to the universe. While there may be a joy in the Stoic's courage, one suspects that there is a higher joy in the passionate will so

[2] Shelley, *Prometheus Unbound.*

to better things that the mere suffering of them will no longer be necessary.

Self-Realization

Finally, there is a third view that has played a large part in our thinking. On the face of it, it seems more reasonable than either of the foregoing. It is the so-called theory of self-realization. The chief business of one's life, according to this view, is to realize oneself.

Doubtless if the view is thought through to its logical end with a full consciousness of all that human life may be, it will serve. But we must first ask what it is that man has in him to realize. That such thinking through is not always successfully accomplished, is witnessed by the fact that the theory leads in many cases to a curious kind of willfulness and to self-gratification.

Suppose, however, we discover that the best that man has in him is this unique ability to go consciously and energetically toward the bringing into being of a better condition. In that case self-realization will mean the highest development in oneself of the power thus to prevision and execute.

Passing from a Static View of Life

It seems that we have here, then, one most essential clue as to what needs to be known about ourselves. We are creatures that have emerged and are still emerging. Only, our emergence need not wait upon the slow processes otherwise prevailing in nature. Our emergence may, to an extent, depend upon ourselves. The most sig-

nificant sense of living, then, will be achieved wherever
this advolutional power becomes manifest.

Little of this was stressed in the older ages. Their
ethics—and they are the ethics in which most of us have
been trained—were chiefly static: the ethics of obedience, decorum, safe behavior. One scarcely finds in the
older moral codes an eager belief in rebelling for a
greater rightness' sake, in taking things intelligently in
hand, in overcoming the irrelevancies and the self-
frustrations of tradition and building anew through the
power of wise thinking. Doubtless this is due to the fact
that the older moral codes date from a period in man's
life when he was quite unconscious of his power to
change the world. His main task, in those older ages,
was to adjust himself to a world already there. In so
doing, he had to learn to live decently with his fellows.
Too much selfishness, too much rancorous hatred, too
much violence would set things in disarray. So he was
sternly commanded in various ways to behave himself.
When he had kept all the commandments, there was little else to do save eat, work, play, and reproduce.

Today, however, our best thought has gone beyond
that static conception of life. It becomes increasingly
clear that what has been is only the starting point for
what is to be. The clarity, however, is, for the most part,
chiefly an intellectual one. It has not yet become incorporated into our behavior patterns—as have honesty, respect for life and property, and sexual fidelity. One suspects that the next step in advance will be taken when
the advolutional quality of human life will be vividly

and persistently part of our total emotional reaction to life.

Inadequacy of the Physical Patterns

Apparently, then, we have here discovered, on our human level, a highly significant process. Perhaps its greatest significance lies in the fact that it discloses a new kind of causality—causality by reference to the future. But the future does not yet exist. Thus it is, in a sense, causality by reference to the non-existent.

Obviously such causality is not found in the physical world. There a particle moves because some other particle has bumped against it. Or it moves because some force has been exerted to make it move. In any event, the particle or the force is an existent reality. When, on the other hand, one projects a plan and moves toward its accomplishment, part of the situation is an unreality.

Inasmuch as the traditional patterns of the physical world have no place in them for such causality, they are inadequate to explain a process which, daily and in millionfold manner, takes place on the human level. Advolution, in brief, requires that we advance beyond the merely physical type of process if we wish a thoroughly inclusive description of reality.

Somehow, in all this, the significant destiny of man begins dimly to be seen—only dimly, indeed, for the ultimate destiny is doubtless beyond us. But dimly we can see man, the curious dreamer of dreams, casting his dreams ahead of him—catching up to them—and again casting them ahead.

Chapter VII

THE SIGNIFICANCE OF THE PSYCHOLOGICAL EMERGENT

THE NEXT AREA OF EXPLORATION

ONE of our distinguished physicists, Professor A. B. Compton, Nobel prize-winner, was reported recently to have said that it may yet turn out to be true that thoughts are the most important things in the world. We may not be sure what was in his mind when he made this statement, but we can perhaps guess from the context. He was recalling the theory of Professor Heisenburg, of Leipzig, that there is an element of indeterminateness in the physical world. That theory, according to Professor Compton, is of far-reaching consequence. If it is true, it disposes of the older belief in the sheer mechanical uniformity of the physical world and opens the way for the entrance of mind into the processes of nature.

Statements like this about the value and power of mental life are being increasingly made by our most responsible thinkers in science. They indicate that the best equipped thought of the times is turning in a new direction. That remarkable genius, Steinmetz, made the prediction shortly before his death that the next significant discoveries would be made in the realms of the mental and the spiritual. Obviously such a prediction could remain only nonsense as long as the belief prevailed that the mental and spiritual were negligible epiphenomena which could really do nothing in a world completely determined by mechanical laws and processes. But that belief no longer predominates. Increasingly the scientist, exploring atomic energies, is coming to the view that these energies do not tell the whole story.

The Psychological Individual

What is the nature of the psychological as it is incorporated in a human individual? What we note, in the first place, is that this psychological individual presents a strange paradox. A physical thing presents no such paradox. The chair in front of me is precisely there where is it. It is there and only there. But I, the psychological being who observes the chair, am not only here in this place in which I am; I am also over there. But also, I am in many other places. I am there at the window. I am outside in the street. Nay, just now, something happens within me, and I am over in London in a certain house in Russell Square. In brief, I, as a creature of mind, have the curious power to be, as it were, in many places at one and the same time.

But I have a further power which physical things do not appear to possess. The chair exists *now*. It is doubtful whether it has at this moment an existence in the past. The traces of the past, indeed, are upon it—it is worn by the usage of the years; but one doubts whether this chair, at the present moment, is brooding reminiscently upon its past. It is likewise doubtful whether the chair can exist effectively in a future. It will indeed, if all goes well, continue into a future time, but the chair itself has no power to anticipate that future, prepare itself against its coming and make plans to meet it.

I, on the contrary, have this curious power to be in more than the *now*. The past actually lives in me. For example, I can remember something that a week ago I promised to do. Re-living that past I can proceed to do what I promised. Also I can live effectively into the future. I can think of tomorrow and of what may then transpire and can organize my life today in such a way as to meet the demands of tomorrow.

All this is so obvious and so much a matter of every-day experience that we rarely give it a second thought. And yet, in truth, are we not here in the presence of a kind of process which is of a wholly unprecedented significance? Why we should ever have belittled the psychological process is one of the curious puzzles of our more recent intellectual history. It is as truly a fact as any fact of which we are aware. But more than that, it is a fact of such outstanding consequence that other facts with which we are acquainted, like physical processes, must be regarded as of secondary import.

A psychological being, in other words, has a space-transcending and time-transcending power unlike anything else that we know in the world. Or to express it differently, such a being has a power of compresence in space and in the past, present, and future of time. There may be foreshadowings of this in the lower organic forms, but they are dim and ineffective compared with the vitality of this power as it occurs on the human level. On the inorganic level we seem, as yet, to find not even foreshadowings.

Here, then, is a reality—as truly factual as atom or protoplasmic cell, a reality, moreover, that has, by reason of the characteristics just described, a creative effectiveness far greater than that which belongs to any other orders.

The Psychological Being as a Unifier

Let us examine the reasons for this greater creativity. An active process of unifying is perhaps most uniquely characteristic of psychological life. The chair *is* a unity, but it does not itself *unify*. I, however, who sit here, form all kinds of unities. In the first place, I hold together all these things around me in the unity of one experience. I call it a room. The chair is *in* this room, but the chair has no awareness of "room." "Room" is the kind of experience-unity that a mental being alone can create. For "room" means recognized relationships between various separate things.

But I also create other unities. I look out of the window, and I create a new unity of experience that includes a passing automobile, a man with a dog, sidewalks, and houses. To be sure, each of these was there before I looked out of the window. But when I looked, I created a unity of experience which was not any of the things I saw. It was a unity that belonged to me.

I return to my writing, and again I create unities. I drag words out of the limbo of possibility and give them a concrete existence on paper. As I set them down they form unities which, in their full context, were never in the world before. This sentence, for example, which I have just written is a new event in nature. Doubtless it is nothing to get greatly excited over, but it is a new event nevertheless. My peculiar unifying process has created this event.

Herein lies the most characteristic power of psychological life. It can, so to speak, reach out in countless ways and bring to itself that out of which it forms its unities. The plant, of course, does this in a limited way. By means of its roots it reaches out to the chemicals of the earth and incorporates them. The plant transforms them into the unity of its metabolic life. But the plant has only a few stereotyped ways of reaching out. The human individual has many ways. Even to begin to enumerate them would be a weariness. Every act of vision is such a reaching out and incorporation of reality to form new unities of experience. Every touching, hearing, smelling, tasting, is of the same kind. Every remembering and every act of thinking about anything means the creation of new unities.

One might say that while the psychological being, in his reaching out, is indeed similar to the plant, he is of far wider power. Nature, in short, in him, has apparently achieved an agency which can function in wider areas than any other form of energy which we know.

It is for this reason, doubtless, that the human being possesses a restlessness and also a progressiveness unknown in other existents. The fact is that he has more of the world open to him. To be sure, he has his own limitations. There are regions of reality that lie as yet utterly outside his contact. Nevertheless, compared with all the creatures or entities we know, the psychological being is the most widely powerful.

Self-Maintenance and Structural Configuration

There is something further to be noted about the human individual. He has self-maintenance and structural configuration.

Thus, for example, mental creatures do not, so to speak, melt into one another. Each is persistently individual. I may go to sleep at night and lose all consciousness, but I can be quite confident that when I awake in the morning I shall not be my son nor my neighbor. I shall still be myself. And, in a profoundly mysterious way, I go on being myself for all the years of my life. There may be moments when I seem to lose track of myself—as in the delirium of a fever. And when death comes I seem to be lost forever. But I recover from the fever and am again my individual self. Whether I recover from death is still our unsolved problem.

There is, in short, a kind of toughness about the

psychological being. He holds on to himself. He has a toughness of individuality similar to that of the atom, which refuses, so to speak, to become any other kind of atom, and similar likewise to the plant, which holds its own and does not become a different plant.

The individual, in other words, shares with all other kinds of reality the fundamental characteristic of self-maintenance.

He also shares the characteristic of structural configuration. We have noted the fact that the atom is no undifferentiated mass, but is a highly structured form of energy. So is the protoplasmic cell. But so likewise is the psychological being. Indeed, a most suggestive parallel might be drawn between him and these other orders of existence. What is most characteristic of him is that he is, as it were, *nucleated*. What I call my self is the central reality which I carry around. Everything that comes within my experience moves, so to speak, around that nucleus of selfhood. From the very first moment in life, when the individual is much like the simple protoplasmic cell, the nucleus is present. There is, even in that first stage, the power to respond as an individual entity to stimuli. The responses become increasingly organized, but in every stage of the process the organizing proceeds around a central psychological nucleus.

Sometimes the nucleus breaks up, and we have a multiple personality. When that happens there is not a proper individual, but something weak, ineffective, and torn to pieces, and our efforts are directed toward restoring the single nucleation that is characteristic of the human being.

Memory and Language

The individual has still another power. He can, so to speak, dissociate himself from the immediacy of his experience and yet hold on to the experience. In other words, he can remember. Animals doubtless can do this to a slight degree, but to so slight a degree that they are unable to compass an efficacy which even the average human individual achieves. The human being can hold on to many memories. This gives him an extended power of comparison not present in creatures who chiefly have one immediate experience after another, each experience being purely transient. The human being, on the other hand, with his capacity for holding many things, actual and remembered, at one and the same time in the unity of his apprehension, can extract from these things their similarities and differences. When, now, he extracts a similarity—for example, out of all the trees he has seen—he can hold this similarity in memory even while he experiences each particular tree. He therefore, in each experience, possesses a double awareness—the awareness of this particular tree and the awareness of the remembered similarity. Thus, each time, he can measure the individual tree against the similarity which he holds in memory. The individual experiences come and go, but the similarity remains permanent.

It is because of this that the human individual can shape his greatest of all tools—language. For language is nothing but the tagging, so to speak, of the similarities that remain permanent in the midst of all the changes of particulars. Thus "horse" is the expression of the similarity that exists in countless horses, "house" the expression of the similarity that exists in countless houses.

This is perhaps the individual's greatest power, for it makes the process of unifying far more effective than it could otherwise be. To say "dog" is to unify innumerable creatures with a single word. No human being could easily carry within himself all the dogs he had seen or was likely to see. By contriving a shorthand expression, "dog," all the thousands of dogs easily take their place within the unity of his experience.

So immeasurably great has been the power resulting from this single process of naming similarities that it is really beyond the compass of description. All science, literature, religion, all effective communication, all planning and carrying out of plans, all business enterprise, all institutions are the outcome of this one power —a power which we find nowhere else in all the realms of nature.

The Reality of the Psychological

If we sum up the foregoing, we come to realize that the psychological individual is a significant form of reality. He is not lightly to be brushed aside. If indeed he seems to fall outside the computabilities of the mechanical world, there may be a reason for that. He may be of an order of reality not reducible to the limited regularities of physical existence. He may demand for his formulation a higher kind of calculus as yet undiscovered.

But in any event, it would seem justifiable to believe that in this kind of being, with his unifying efficacy, his toughness of self-maintenance, his definite nucleation, his highly structured organization, and his power of memory and language, we have a reality which, far from being negligible, is the source of the most actively creative processes we know. We find in him much that is similar to the protoplasmic and the atomic types of being, but enough that is different to cause us to believe that in emerging to the psychological level, nature has come to operate in ways more widely and progressively effective than on any other levels of which we are as yet aware.

Chapter VIII

THINGS AS MANIFESTATIONS

AN APPROACH TO THE INVISIBLE

WE have all felt the baffling inadequacy of our understanding of things. Mysteries encompass us on every hand. They are apparently beyond our knowing. Perhaps there is a certain defensive necessity about this. If we desire to live with some measure of success, we must keep alert within the immediate area of our human concerns. And yet there is a teasing sense that beyond that area is a reality we should love to know.

Two attitudes have been taken toward this "beyond." One is that it is inevitably and forever beyond. Ultimate Reality, as Spencer believed, is unknowable. Kant expressed the same view in his peculiar phraseology: we can never know the "thing-in-itself" (*Ding an sich*), but only reality as it appears to us. It appears to us under the guise of time, space, and the categories of the human mind. These are like lenses through which we must look. Because we are human, we can never take off the lenses. So we are forever barred from coming face to face with the ultimate mysteries.

There is, on the other hand, the attitude which we were describing in a previous chapter. Knowledge is a process of adding point of view to point of view. There is one sense, indeed, in which we can never completely know anything that is other than ourselves. Let us recall the case of Richard Jones. To know the real man, we concluded, one would have to multiply all the possible points of view from which he might be regarded. But one of them is that of Richard Jones himself. Hence to know this individual completely one would have to be the man himself. This was the puzzling conclusion reached by the mystic philosopher, Plotinus. Knowledge of the Real must disappear into actually *being* the Real.

We need not pursue the matter into this puzzling region. It is perhaps sufficient to admit that as one does attempt to regard an individual from all possible points of view, one comes increasingly near to the identification of oneself with that individual. Thus the mother who attempts to solve her child's difficulties, not by rigorously maintaining her adult standpoint, but by putting herself as best she can at the point of view of the child, does, in a sense, become the child. As, in that limited sense, she becomes the child, she opens a door into a reality that for the most part is closed.

Doors are usually closed among us—closed on pretty nearly everything and everyone. Or, more accurately, they are almost entirely closed. We know individuals and things from a few points of view. We seldom make the effort to achieve all the points of view that are possible. Thus in large measure, by our limitation of point of view, we are indeed shut out from reality. But this is not because there is some impenetrable wall between ourselves and the Real, but because, for one reason or another, we do not sufficiently compass all the points of view that are available.

It was Hegel who grasped this. He denied Kant's assumption that reality is unreachably beyond us in a domain locked against our entrance. We live, he said, in a world of unreality only insofar as we live in a world of partial standpoints. The real destiny of the mind is to reach completeness of point of view. The reason for all life-frustration is incompleteness—the inability to be wholly in and of the situation. Sin, for example, is a setting up of one's partial wish as if it were the whole. Error is acting upon one's partial insight as if it were the totality. The chief end of life, then, is to overcome partialness. The whole process of history, according to Hegel—in the degree that history is significant—is one of passing beyond incomplete points of view into those that are less incomplete.

There is something singularly stimulating about such an attitude. If it is true, we need not conceive of ourselves as baffled creatures, beating vainly against doors into reality that will not open. It may be, indeed, that we can at best only open small doors into small vistas. But at any rate they open into something. We are not stopped at the outset by a metaphysical "No Admittance." And apparently the more doors we open, the fuller our view of that something becomes.

Opening One Door

There is one door into reality that is not difficult to open; and yet, for the most part, it remains
closed.

In the main, we are creatures who see "things." We
see what we see and usually not beyond what we see.
To experience the world as merely a world of things is
doubtless to fail of something that is significant. The
experience of things, to be sure, is good as far as it goes.
It enables us to move about our world and to manipulate the life-factors with some success. Most persons
would be adept at naming the things around them—
mountains, rivers, trees, houses, automobiles. But for
the most part they would sense nothing but the things
themselves. They would remain, so to speak, at the
physical surfaces.

It is possible, however, to get a different "feel" of
one's world if one is able to develop another habit of
mind. It is, in short, the habit of seeing the invisible in
the visible reality; the habit of penetrating surfaces,
of seeing through things to their initiating sources.

One must, to be sure, start at the right end. It will
not do to look at a mountain, or a star, and seek to
penetrate to its initiating source. One will either be
baffled and say nothing, or one will say the unilluminating word "God"—unilluminating, because it is an
indication simply of a vague wonder and an unsolved
mystery. Mountains and stars are still too far removed
for us to be able to say what their initiating sources

are. One sees their ways of operation, but no more. One must therefore begin with what is nearer at hand.

In the Midst of Invisible Powers

Let us start with the room in which one sits. It has tables, chairs, lamps, and shelves of books. One sits comfortably among these things. If a friend comes in one might expect him to remark upon the delightful arrangement. One might not be surprised if he walked up to the shelves and fingered the volumes. One might, however, be somewhat astonished, if, having opened a volume or two, and having seated himself, he should suddenly remark that it was curious how calmly one could sit in the midst of invisible powers. One might glance about a little curiously. Where were the invisible powers?

He would have little difficulty in explaining himself. Every book, he might say, is the outer form or embodiment of a wish to express something. The book seems, indeed, to be nothing but paper, print and cloth, but back of it is a need, a wish, and a whole organized process of thought. The book is visible, but these—the initiators of the book—are invisible.

Once one learns the art of thus penetrating beyond surfaces, most of the things around us take on strangely new life. The chair, for example, on which one sits is not simply a dead thing. Back of it is a human need— to rest one's body. That is the "why" of the chair. Back of it also is the first inventive thought that came to its

fruition in this type of device. And back of this particular chair are the plans of the designer, the conscious
application of the craftsman, the selective taste of the
merchant, and the further selective taste of the buyer.
The chair, in short, is a focussing point of a whole series
of conscious activities. If it is, indeed, itself a non-living
thing, it is at least the visible manifestation or embodiment of what is far from dead.

We live, in short, in the midst of invisible powers. A
city, to a thing-minded person, is streets, houses, banks,
telegraph poles, parks, automobiles, and the rest. To
the person who penetrates through the things to their
initiating causes, it is a thousandfold expression of
needs, desires, plannings, and conscious executions.
These are the essential city. Without them it could
never have come into being. Take this particular building. It is a postoffice. Looked at superficially, it is
stones, glass, steel, wood. But looked at with an eye to
its initiating reality, it is the outcome of a fundamental
need. The postoffice exists because there is the need
among us to communicate with one another at a distance. Remove that need, and the postoffice is a meaningless heap of stones. There is, in that case, no sense
in it. It is merely an encumbrance. Again, take a schoolhouse. It, too, is the manifestation or embodiment of a
need, the need systematically to orientate young people
in the life-situation in which they find themselves.
Schoolhouses did not exist among primitive people and
do not exist among animals because the need was and
is absent. Once the need is felt, however, the bricks,

wood, glass, and blackboards come together by a kind
of inevitability.

In this sense, it is the need that is the creative factor
in the situation. Bricks, wood, glass, and blackboards
have no power to gather themselves together into
schoolhouses. They are themselves means, and the physical schoolhouse is itself simply a resultant.

Every man-made thing, then, is a manifestation of
what we might call psychological causality. The need is
the initiating force. For it is the need that starts things
going, and it is the conscious thought in response to need
that brings them to the wished-for completion.

A city is need expressed or manifested in various outer
forms. The outer forms, to the discerning mind, are not
independent, self-sustaining realities. They are the ways
in which the needs are realized. These outer forms, then,
are a kind of language. As we walk the streets of a city,
we can read the language. An automobile? The outer
form taken in response to man's need for swift and easy
locomotion. A department store? The outer form taken
in response to man's need for exchange of commodities.

At the time of writing this a fleet of warships has
steamed up the Hudson. It also speaks a language.
Groups of men, called nations, apparently still feel the
need to be suspicious of one another and on occasion to
fight one another. On Fifth Avenue, in New York, is a
building called the "Peace House." In its brick-and-
mortar language, it tells of another kind of need. Or, on
a train, one rides through the outskirts of a city and
passes in the rear of houses. There, again, one finds a

various language spoken. One yard is a hideous mass of unassorted junk; another is neatly plotted with flowers. In each case the outer form is the expression of something invisible but real. One may safely predict what manner of psychological causality is present in the occupants of these two houses. In other words, while it is true that one passes by physical things called yards, one is far more truly passing by attitudes, desires, and wishes. These cannot be seen by the eye. They must be apprehended by something in us that can grasp the invisible initiating powers that produce these things.

Seeing Through the Visible

Obviously it is this ability to grasp the invisible that makes us intelligent about our man-made world. May we surmise that it is that ability which alone can, if ever, make us intelligent about the world beyond the man-made?

Let us suppose that an infant is wheeled down a city street. An automobile goes by. The mother who wheels the baby has an instant understanding of what has passed. She knows what it is because she knows why it is; that is, she knows the need which it serves. But for the baby the automobile is doubtless only a swift visual blur. The mother, in other words, can do more than see with her eyes. She can penetrate beyond the seeing to the unseeable need that the vehicle fulfils. The child, on the other hand, can as yet only see with its eyes. It is still, as we say, merely at the stage of sense-power.

Later the child will come to understand what an automobile is. But as long as the child remains wholly at the level of its sense-power, that understanding is impossible.

One can illustrate this by reference to a foreign language. The reader may have had the baffling experience of traveling in a country of whose language he was in total ignorance. The sense reports which he received may have been perfect. He may have been able to hear every sound; he may also have been able to see lips move and hands gesticulate. As a creature of sensation, in short, he was all that was to be desired. But, as long as he could not penetrate beyond the hearing and the seeing to the invisible and the unheard, in other words, to the meaning of the words, he was completely baffled; he was on the outside.

All these man-made things, like houses, automobiles, and the rest, are, we have said, a language which, after our few years of infancy, we understand. Why are we able to understand? Because these things are obviously there in response to needs that we ourselves have and therefore can comprehend. But beyond the man-made things there is a vast physical world of things not made by man—mountains, rivers, meadows, stars, planets. It is here that our understanding falters and fails. We can apprehend these only from the outside, that is, as *objects of sense*. If they indeed speak a language, it is like the foreign language that we do not understand, or the sense-flash of the automobile that to the infant is only a blur of vision.

Our scientific approach to these things of the world

beyond the man-made is, as we know, wholly on the
level of sense perception. On that level, we are able to
learn all manner of important facts about these things—
their structure and their correlations with other things;
but we are apparently no more able to learn their meaning than we should be to learn the meaning of an automobile if we could simply observe its outer appearance
and had no opportunity whatever to connect its complicated structure with the needs which that structure was
created to fulfil.

Can We Penetrate Beyond the Man-Made?

This brings us to an arresting thought, one which we
must express with the greatest care lest it be misinterpreted. From our knowledge of the relation of man-
made things to creative needs, it would seem that we
should go singularly wrong if we supposed that because
we were unable to read the meaning of the language of
those outer things of the universe there was no meaning
to it, that stars, planets, mountains, and the rest, down
to the elementary atoms, were simply meaningless
"things." There would seem to be at least a presumption in favor of the view that wherever there is external
reality, some invisible power has in it been made manifest.

To be sure, we should go equally wrong if we leaped
to a swift conclusion about this invisible creative reality,
investing it at once with a certain describable nature.
That has been the error of man in all the ages. Out of

altogether insufficient knowledge, he built him images of the cosmic creative powers—Isis, Osiris, Thor, Odin, Jupiter, Shiva, and the rest. These were to him the creators of the non-man-made things. But even if we reject all these misconceptions, we should still seem justified in believing that the world of physical reality is not itself an ultimate, but that back of it, so to speak, is the initiating energy which organizes it into these particular forms. The profounder reality of the world, in other words, if it is ever to be discovered, will doubtless not be found on its sense-perceptible surfaces, but beyond these in some creative power.

This is the question of all questions, and we have no right in these critical modern days to be dogmatic. The foregoing simply suggests a possibility. There can be no doubt of what we find among our man-made things. Psychological causality—the causality, that is, springing out of need—is so fundamental that without it they would simply not have come to be. Whether we can extend this thought beyond the man-made is of course a most perplexing question. We can, of course, in a way, extend it *below* the man-made. We may suspect that the bird's nest is built in response to some dimly felt need, even though that need may not rise to the level that we call consciousness. In this case, the outer or physical must be regarded as a resultant. The power is not in it, but in something, so to speak, creatively back of it. Even if we express animal life in terms of tropisms, the external things are still the effects of invisible powers.

Whether we can extend the thought above the man-made is the most difficult of all questions.[1] What are these incredibly vast physical masses that move in the heavens with a regularity and a power beyond our comprehension? The psalmist could say: "The heavens declare the glory of God." We hesitate to use such language today. But can we, with any claim to intelligibility say: "The heavens declare themselves to be simply masses of matter"? Then the heavens, in that case, are even lower in reality than man-made things. For man-made things at least declare the glory of needs that can triumphantly win their way to fulfilment.

The Reality of the Psychological

We do find in the world with which we are intimately acquainted a type of causality that is not physical. To say that this non-physical causality is confined only to a small corner of the universe—to the world of human beings—does not signify much. For if there actually is non-physical or psychological causality, then there it is. It belongs to the world of reality, which means that this is one way in which the world of reality operates. Our only question, then, is how widely it operates. Is the world a blind movement of physical entities, or is the entire physical world, in a manner that we do not now understand, subject to initiating powers that are other than physical? The small door we are able to open upon our

---

[1] "Phenomena come to us disguised in their frame-works of time and space; they are messages in cipher of which we shall not understand the ultimate significance until we have discovered how to decode them out of their space-time wrappings." Jeans, Sir James, *The Universe Around Us*, p. 319 (Macmillan).

human world, indeed, does not open up the full expanse
of the universe, but it at least suggests possibilities. We
do know psychological causality, we do experience things
wrought into being out of response to needs and through
the power of conscious planning. It is at least unjusti-
fiable, then, to say that the psychological is unreal. In
our man-made world it is the most real power we know
—far more real (even though these are indispensable)
than bricks or stone or steel. For without the psychological
they would be utterly meaningless and would never come
to exist in the particular organized forms in which we
know them. The psychological is the reason for their being and the justification for their continuance.

The Reality of Mind

Let us return once more to Eddington. The physicist,
who deals expertly with the external world, should at
least have his say. What he says in this case, however,
turns out to be surprisingly in the vein of our conjec-
tures. For, writes Eddington, "actuality is not susceptible
of definition without trespassing beyond the frontiers of
physics. . . . If we consider a world entirely devoid
of consciousness (as we frequently try to do) there is, as
far as we know, no meaning whatever in discriminating
between the worlds A and B. The mind is a referee who
decides in favor of A against B. We cannot describe the
difference without referring to a mind. The actuality
of the world is a spiritual value. The physical world at
some point (or indeed throughout) impinges on the

spiritual world and derives its actuality solely from this contact." [2]

Those are impressive words for a physicist to utter. But still more impressive are to come. "We have attempted in this essay to show the direction in which, it appears to us, the tendency of modern scientific thought is leading. It differs markedly from the views of thirty years ago. . . . Our thesis has been that the recent tendencies of scientific thought lead to the belief that mind is a greater instrument than was formerly recognized in prescribing the nature and laws of the external world as studied in physical science; that in exploring his own territory the physicist comes up against the influence of that wider reality which he cannot altogether shut out. . . . We have spelled mind with a small 'm,' for our values are human values; yet we trust there is even in us something that has value for the eternal. Perhaps the actuality of the world is not only in these little sparks from the divine mind which flicker for a few years and are gone, but in the Mind, the Logos. 'The same was in the beginning with God . . . and without Him was not anything made that was made.' " [3]

Finding a Kinship

Of what use, it may be asked, is all this kind of thinking? At best it seems to leave us only with a very large question mark. But perhaps it does something more.

[2] Eddington, "The Domain of Science." In Needham, *Science, Religion and Reality*, p. 211 (Macmillan).
[3] *Ibid.*, p. 217.

The habit of seeing things as manifestations, of seeing the outer as expressions of initiating powers hidden from our eyes, may reduce for us the usual opacity of the world. For thing-minded persons the world is opaque. Their eyes, indeed, see, but they do not see *through*. For those of us, on the other hand, who see things in the way we have indicated, things become singularly transparent. We look through them to their initiating causes. And when we do that the world becomes incredibly alive.

Even a city becomes strangely alive when we read its language of needs, desires, aspirations, frustrations, triumphs. May not the wider world in like manner become alive if we read its outer things—stars, planets, mountains, rivers—as the manifestations of invisible creative powers that are akin to the psychological powers we possess? What those invisible powers are we do not know; but that they are, of this we would seem to be assured. The brute opacity of the external world is thus broken through. The heavens declare the glory of something alive and creative.

"This does not lead us to power," writes Tagore,[4] "as knowledge does, but it gives us joy, which is the product of the union of kindred things." There is a fine wisdom in that sentence. To be an alien is to be unhappy. The greatest happiness lies in the realization of a fundamental kinship.

As we have realized in the more recent decades, there is nothing particularly joyous in an outcast relation to the universe. That relation may be the only one which is

[4] *Sādhanā*, p. 8 (Macmillan).

open to us, and, if so, we shall have to accept it. But if the truth is that we have ourselves, by our own inadequate hypotheses, created our outcast relation in the universe, then we have merely, through our own erroneous thinking, devised needless tragedy for ourselves. It may be that what we find so powerfully in ourselves is not unlike what is powerfully in the universe. In other words, it may be that there is a fundamental kinship between ourselves and the creative world in which we live. "If this possibility were an actuality, if there truly were at the heart of nature something akin to us, a conserver and increaser of values, and if we could not only know this and act upon it, but really feel it, life would suddenly become radiant. For no longer should we be alien accidents in an indifferent world, uncharacteristic by-products of the blindly whirling atoms; and no longer would the things that matter most be at the mercy of the things that matter least." [5] We could, then, as our Indian poet writes, "hail the morning sun, the flowing water, the fruitful earth, as the manifestation of the same living truth which holds us in its embrace." We could become united with something that is not dead but greatly alive.

[5] W. P. Montague, *Belief Unbound*, p. 7 (Yale University Press). This is a brilliant attempt, in the spirit of modern science and philosophy, to formulate a new basis for religion.

Part Three

THE GREAT ELEMENTALS

There the Eternals are, and there
The Good, the Lovely, and the True,
And Types, whose earthly copies were
The foolish broken things we knew.

RUPERT BROOKE

Chapter IX

THE PHILOSOPHIC TEST

THE CRITERION OF ACTABILITY

IN Part One of this book we tried to reorientate ourselves with regard to our ways of thinking. We recognized that great as the achievements of the modern centuries had been—scientifically and technologically there had been no such centuries in the whole history of man—they had left us, nevertheless, as to the major matters of our concern, in an unsatisfactory condition. Physics had invited us to look to the atom for our most important illumination; biology, to the protoplasmic cell and the lower animal orders. While indeed the illumination that we thus achieved was very real, there was much that induced in us a considerable dismay. We were aware that to be dismayed was no indication of the untruth of what dismayed us. Indeed, we learned to take the scientific sentence pronounced upon us without even so much as a protest. Nevertheless it was a drastic sentence, for it deprived us of that which, in our civilized history, we had prized most greatly of all: our sense of significance.

By the end of the nineteenth century, we were left with a heritage of ideas that turned the living universe into a dead one, a meaningful universe into a meaningless one, a spiritual universe into a mechanical one, a universe forever new into one that endlessly repeated the already-there, our minds into epiphenomena, and ourselves into tailless animals adrift in a cosmos too huge to concern itself with us—if indeed it had the power to concern itself with anything at all.

In reviewing that heritage of ideas we seemed to find traces in it of gravely fallacious thinking. We noted chiefly the fallacy of abstraction, or of "misplaced concreteness," which consisted of concentrating upon one aspect of reality and pronouncing that one aspect the whole.

We also noted a second fallacy, that of regarding the earlier in development as the more real and therefore the more important. Because of this genetic fallacy we had been bidden to pattern ourselves upon our forebears, despite the fact that we ourselves seemed to have advanced considerably beyond their primitive status.

There seemed also to be another fallacious way of thinking. We might call it the fallacy of black-white thinking. Because our anthropomorphic-minded ancestors created naïve gods, we were admonished that every trace of the mental and the spiritual must be eliminated from the universe. It was a case of accepting either their ridiculous spiritual reality or no spiritual reality at all. The choice was an embarrassing one to have to make, and as no one wished to be found in the company of those misconceived gods and goddesses, most of us joined the ranks of those who claimed deadness for their portion.

We are now, however, able to think with a little more

discrimination. The twentieth-century physical scientist frankly acknowledges the limitations of his inquiry, and himself warns us against committing the fallacy of abstraction; the emergent evolutionist reverses the attitude adopted by the genetic fallacy and claims the later-evolved as the more significant. Both of these attitudes, taken together, make the drastic choice demanded of us by black-white thinking no longer necessary. Even though we sweep the heavens with our telescopes and find no living being there, we are now assured that telescopes only explore the surfaces of the world. The physical, we are told, impinges upon a wider reality which the physical sciences are themselves powerless to explore.

Man a Revealer

In Part Two we took counsel with this more discriminating thought and deliberately abandoned the old procedures. We suggested that, valuable as the physical and biological explorations had been and would remain, we should do ill to neglect the exploration of that type of reality in which nature had apparently reached a more advanced level of functioning—the level of human life. Why, we asked, might we not assume that human life could be as revealing of nature, if not more so, than the animal and the atomic orders? It seemed at least worth while to attempt to discover the processes on the human level that appeared to be significant.

In pursuing this method we detected in evolution on

the human level a purposed movement toward more widely functioning wholes. This gave us ground to believe that to call nature completely purposeless was simply loose thinking. We detected also a form of evolution peculiar to man, a form in which the individual or group consciously moves toward a preconceived end instead of unconsciously evolving from the past. We detected also in mind a type of initiating power unlike anything to be found elsewhere in nature and with so amazing an effectiveness that it could not cavalierly be brushed aside. Finally, we seemed to discover a kind of clue to the understanding of the external world. Starting with our man-made world, we discovered that things were manifestations of invisible creative powers. The latter were in no sense mysterious, but were, as we discovered, psychological in nature. As a result, we surmised that all external reality might, in some sense, be a similar manifestation of invisible creative powers.

The method we adopted would seem to have met with a fair degree of success. The human processes, we seemed justified in concluding, apparently do reveal something of the reality we are seeking to know.

A Deeper Inquiry

We have been repeatedly using the word "reality," taking it in its rough-and-ready meaning. We must now attempt to invest the word with a greater precision. For reality is apparently the key-word of all philosophic inquiry. The misunderstanding of its meaning, as we shall presently see, has doubtless been the source of the major errors of human thinking.

What, then, do we mean by reality?

Suppose I have a dream that I have suddenly come into possession of a million dollars. I wake up, a good deal disappointed, and call the dream an unreality. Why do I call it an unreality? The dream itself was real enough. All my dream exuberance was real enough. And my present disappointment is distressingly real. Apparently, then, there is a good deal of reality there; nevertheless I call the dream unreal.

What I mean is that the total scheme of things which the dream implied cannot be acted out. If the dream were reality I should now be investing in many things that I have long desired to have—a high-powered car, world travel, and other delights. But should I attempt to purchase those things, I should find myself in considerable financial difficulties.

Reality, then, in this sense, is that which can be acted out. We call the fantasies of the insane unrealities. Again, in themselves, they are real enough, but in the total scheme of actions which they imply, they are unreal. Thus the megalomaniac who insists that he has written a dozen books that are best sellers would find himself hard pushed to it to point out those volumes in the bookstores. His statement, in short, cannot be acted out to the end. We call a mirage an unreality. Again, *as* a mirage —that is, as a particular image on one's retina—it is real. But it is unreal so far as what it seems to indicate is concerned. It seems to indicate a lake, and it suggests, to the desert traveler, that if he goes to it he will find water to slake his thirst. The traveler may for a while be taken in by the unreality, but as soon as he acts on all that it implies, he finds himself misled. The situation, in short, simply will not act out.

In a preceding chapter, we tried to indicate the "unreality" of the thing-minded person's attitude toward the things of his world. If, we pointed out, he were fully to act out what each thing implied, he would find not simply the thing, as a kind of entity-in-itself, but the needs and desires out of which the thing sprang. In order, then, to get a "real" view of his world of things, he would have to go back through the whole scheme of action which the thing implied to the initiating factors which brought it into being.

The Tests to Apply

What, then, in this world, is "reality," and how can it be found? The simplest answer is that reality is what can be acted out, and the way to find it is to act it out.

Is two plus two equals four a reality? Try it and see. Is good faith a reality? Try it and see. Is persistent lying a reality? Again, the proof is in the trying. If persistent deception works, with a continuous and unbroken effectiveness, it must be accounted a reality. Of course, in one sense, it *is* a reality. That is, each act of deception, as a psychological happening, is a reality. But what is implied in an act of deception is that this is a way of successful life. It is this implication which is either a reality or an unreality. The test is "try it and see." In this particular case, man has rejected lying as an "unreal" way of life, for he has seemed to find that in the long run it really does not work.

There are lesser realities and greater realities. The chair, let us say, is a lesser reality. We call it lesser because it involves a scheme of action that plays a small part in life, one that is narrowly limited in its area and therefore in its significance. The law of moving masses, on the other hand, is one of the greater realities because it involves our behavior in countless relationships. We have, so far as physical things are concerned, always to act in terms of that law. Its reality is attested by the fact that whenever we act "gravitationally," so far as the physical factors are concerned we act with success. Whenever we go counter to the gravitational implications, as when we step nonchalantly off a precipice, we meet with disaster. In the latter case, we have tried to act out an unreality and have failed.

Philosophy, in making its search for Reality, is seeking that type which is as inclusive as can be conceived. It does not thereby rule out the lesser realities. It simply recognizes them as more circumscribed in their areas and therefore in their significance. It is seeking for reality in its most universal forms.

How, now, in terms of the above description of reality as actability will philosophy set about its task? The answer is simple: it will seek to find that which in every circumstance of our life can be acted out and must be acted out if life is to be carried on with the most enduring success. Let us suppose that philosophy concludes that Reality is matter. It is saying to us, in effect, that if we will act in every circumstance and toward everything in the way implied by matter, we shall act successfully. In short, it says, the universe as matter is an actable proposition and we shall do best if we act in all ways that matter implies.

The test, again, lies in trying to do that. But as soon as I try to do that, I get into difficulties. If I treat you simply as a piece of matter—that is, as something which merely has space-filling qualities—you will soon resent what I do. For I shall have to disregard your wishes, needs, aspirations, all your friendly attitudes, your loves and dislikes. I cannot find these filling space, and therefore, if I am to act out this proposition, I must take no note of them. But you cry out in protest that they are real, in fact that they are the realest reality in you. If now, in my earnest effort to carry out what the proposition implies, I ruthlessly continue to disregard them, you will become angry, withdraw from my presence, or lay violent hands upon me. If, now, constrained by your agitation, I assure you that hereafter I shall take note of them, but that they all really *are* matter, I am of course saying a meaningless thing, for they are not matter in any sense in which anyone understands matter.

The proposition, in short, cannot be acted out. And therefore we must conclude that there is something wrong with the proposition. What is here called Reality—matter—may indeed be *a* reality—that is, it may be acted out up to a certain limit—but it apparently cannot be regarded as the inclusive or all-embracing form of reality.

Suppose, on the other hand, philosophy says that Reality is mind. Trying to act out that proposition, I shall not get into such great difficulties—at least with you. But there still will be difficulties. With you I shall be on fairly successful terms. If I act toward you always on the supposition that you are mind, I shall never treat you as a stick or a stone. I shall not ruthlessly brush you aside as if you were an encumbrance in my path. I shall treat you as a thinking, considering being. I shall make sure that I know what you are thinking about, and I shall try to understand and address myself to your thinking. All of which will be very much to the good and will make my relation to you a happy and fruitful one.

But when I try to treat my desk as a mind I am in a considerable quandary. Either mind, here, means something that I really do not understand, or if it means mind in the sense that I do understand it, I am at a loss to know what to do. I cannot talk familiarly with my desk. I cannot go into conference with it and ask its opinion on a certain crucial emergency that has arisen. And if I wish to move it from one place in the room to another, it hardly helps for me to ask if its feelings will be hurt by the transfer. No, there may be some meaning in that statement that Reality is mind, but for the life of me I cannot fully act it out. I am at a standstill. So— perhaps with some reluctance—I must believe that the proposition is not entirely true.

Yet the reader is aware that for centuries philosophers have held either the one or the other view. Indeed, most of the controversy in philosophy has been over these two views. Nevertheless a simple test such as we have applied indicates that neither view is really comprehensive.

Philosophy, in brief, has hitherto failed, for the most part, to use this simplest and yet severest of all tests. It has chiefly sought Reality by trying to *think* it. Now it is quite possible to think out a fairly complete scheme of things which nevertheless has no relation—or very little relation—to reality. Lewis Carroll thought out such a scheme in "Alice in Wonderland." But neither Lewis Carroll nor anyone else ever tried to act out the kind of "reality" implied in "Alice in Wonderland." We call such a world the world of fairyland. Fairyland is a realm that makes no demand upon actability. It asks only for thinkability. If you can think of creatures an inch high, with wings and other delectable appurtenances, you can conceive a perfectly thinkable world. But try to live as if that world existed, and you will doubtless end ignobly in an asylum.

Shall we say that philosophy in the past has too largely confined itself to thinkability and so has produced accounts of Reality that are often as far removed from the real as Alice and her adventures? Science, on the other hand, has taken actability for its criterion. The crucial turn was made when Galileo challenged the Aristotelian dictum about falling bodies. Heavier bodies, said Aristotle, fall faster than lighter bodies because of an inherent "heaviness." But he had said that because he had simply *thought* it. And succeeding philosophers accepted his thought, for it seemed obvious. That is, there was nothing in the thought itself that was self-contradictory. Galileo, distrusting the thought, proceeded to act out the proposition. He went to the top of the tower and dropped two unequal weights. Instantly he discovered that the Aristotelian thought, while perfectly thinkable, was utterly unactable. Both weights dropped in the same time.

Applying the Test in Philosophy

How shall we turn from thinkability as a test and develop philosophy on the basis of actability? Philosophy is a search for Reality. In other words, it is a search for the universal conditions of life. Philosophy seeks to know what kind of a world it is in which we live, what we can do in that world, and what we ought to do if life is to compass its fullest possibilities. How is philosophy to succeed in the venture? The answer, it would seem, is that the true function of philosophy is to find—if we may coin so clumsy a word—the great actabilities. It is, in other words, to discover those ways of life which, when acted out, bring an enduring effectiveness.

"The mystery of life," writes Van Der Leeuw, "is not a problem to be solved, it is a reality to be experienced." [1] What, as philosophers, we seek, then, are those fundamental experiences in which reality reveals itself, not as an abstract thought in our head, but as a concrete process of life.

[1] *The Conquest of Illusion*, p. 11 (Knopf).

Chapter X

THE FIRST ELEMENTAL: TRUTH

REALITY AND THE TRUTH-PROCESS

WE are brought, however, to a sudden halt. For there is the type of philosophy which denies that there are any great ways of life that can be consistently acted out. Pessimism in its various forms declares that however confidently we may go into the business of living, the end of it all is frustration. "But in this world . . . man lies under an inescapable sentence of defeat; and in this world . . . all nobility, all happiness, and all high endeavor stay unattainable through the whim of the creator of the world." [1] Nobility, in short, admirable as it may seem, cannot be acted out. Somewhere along the line of life it gets thwarted. Happiness cannot be acted out. High endeavor cannot. Thus, in a profound sense, they are unrealities, illusions. And they are illusions, according to the writer—and to many philosophers—because the universe will not permit them to be acted out.

Another writer expresses this thought with a finality of conviction: "Thinking of Cronshaw, Philip remembered the Persian rug which he had given him, telling

---

[1] Guy Holt, Introduction to Cabell's *Beyond Life*, p. xix (Modern Library).

him that it offered an answer to his question upon the
meaning of life; and suddenly the answer occurred to
him. . . . The answer was obvious. Life had no meaning. On the earth, satellite of a star speeding through
space, living things had arisen under the influence of
conditions which were part of the planet's history; and
as there had been a beginning of life upon it, so, under
the influence of other conditions, there would be an end:
man, no more significant than other forms of life, had
come not as the climax of creation but as a physical reaction to the environment. . . . Life was insignificant
and death without consequence. In the vast warp of
life . . . there was no meaning . . . and nothing was
important." [2]

If all that is true, the relation between ourselves and
the universe can hardly be a friendly one. To have been
brought into existence with the power to develop desires
for many things beautiful and high, and then, for no
reason for which we are accountable, to be condemned
to defeat, would seem to bespeak either a sheer irrationality or an extreme of cruelty in the scheme of things.

> "You gave me wings to fly;
> Then took away my sky." [3]

It is a view that bears investigating. At the very outset, however, we are arrested in our course. *We ourselves, the accusers of the universe, are then greater than
the universe?* For we, at least, have justice in our hearts.

[2] W. Somerset Maugham, *Of Human Bondage*, p. 657 (Modern
Library).
[3] Leonora Speyer, *Fiddler's Farewell*, p. 87 (Knopf).

We would not act this way to any living creature. But since we are in and of the universe, born out of it and inseparably part of it, we might ask in some perplexity how we came to grow this fine flower of justice, if, in the basic scheme of things, justice has no place whatever.

But let us apply our test. Let us take the first possibility, that the universe is utterly irrational. By that we mean that irrationality is the fundamental reality, and rationality is an illusion. Let us try, now, to act out irrationality by being in every possible circumstance utterly irrational. One can at once predict the outcome. To act irrationally is almost instantly to court disaster. Suppose that one denies, in his action, the law of identity, which is the fundamental principle of rationality. The law of identity means that a thing is itself and not not itself. The fire is burning in the hearth. Bent on acting irrationally, one declares, "Fire is not fire," and forthwith plunges one's hand into the flames. Or suppose one insists that two plus two equal fifteen and proceeds to add up one's bank deposits along those irrational lines. Irrationality cannot be acted out. Far from being the ultimate reality, then, it would seem to be the ultimate unreality.

Or suppose, to take the second possibility, that we regard the scheme of things as incredibly cruel. Let us try to act out cruelty. We quickly note that it is a type of behavior which can maintain itself only with the greatest difficulty. Even when one is, with some success, extremely cruel one must make exceptions. One cannot be cruel to those upon whose protection one depends in order to carry out one's cruelty. As soon, in short, as one universalizes cruel behavior—is cruel to everyone under all circumstances—cruelty brings defeat. Cruelty, in other words, is another type of behavior that will not bear acting out. Apparently there is that in the nature of things which rejects it. Thus, if our test is a veritable one, cruelty is not, in an ultimate and enduring sense, a reality, but rather, in that same enduring sense, an unreality.

Plato and the Scientists

That ancient civilization which produced so much which we admire and love—the civilization of the Greeks —held three realities supreme: the True, the Beautiful, and the Good. Plato, master-spokesman of the Greeks, set these "in the heavens" as eternal and all-governing. By this he meant that they were the inescapable and everlasting conditions of everything that is, was, and can be. Whatever achievements there were in life which were worthwhile were adumbrations of these realities. Thus there were in human life more or less fragmentary bits of truth, beauty and goodness—fragmentary, but still reflecting in some small degree the governing realities. Human life might indeed go wrong. It might be ignorant, ugly, and unjust. But it was so, according to this Platonic belief, not because of anything basically at fault in the universe, but rather because human life was as yet unable fully to measure up to the enduring patterns of Truth, Beauty, and Goodness.

Shall we, with our more realistic modern insight, say that Plato was an uncritical optimist, and that, had he

lived in our contemporary society and looked at life
and the universe with a more searching eye, he would
have substituted for the immortal three, a more sophisticated trilogy of the Irrational, the Bad, and the Ugly?
Perhaps. And yet perhaps not. For he doubtless would
have been the first to wax enthusiastic over the basic faith
of the modern scientist in what the scientist calls "the
uniformity of nature." He would have waxed equally
enthusiastic over the scientist's confident belief in his
actual ability to discover truth about things. The scientist,
he would have said, is a truth-believer, nay, one might
say, a truth-worshiper. His whole life is devoted to a
finding of what is veritable, while his every technique
is devoted to the detection and elimination of what is not
true. The scientist, he might have said, not only believes
that there is truth, but that its discovery is the paramount
issue of life.

So Plato would have joined hands with the scientists
as fellows-in-reverence before the first of the Greek
trinity. Whatever pessimistic thinkers may declare, he
might have said, science itself is a way of life based on
an unshakable belief in the truth-structure of the universe. Science cannot deny that belief without denying
itself. For what pertinence could there be in exploring
if there were nothing true to find; what value in elim-
inating error if truth itself were merely an illusion?

Logic in the Universe

But our faith in the truth-seeking process is a persistent one, and it is doubtful whether we should be will-

ing to go so far as to abandon that exhilarating and re-
warding adventure.

What, now, does the truth-seeking process imply?
When we examine what we mean by it—(we shall probably differ from Plato's view of Truth as a pattern)—
we see that it implies something fundamental both to
the universe and to our own part in it. The full implication of the truth-seeking process was late in developing
among mankind. And yet even primitive man seems to
have had a slight sense of what it was. As he learned to
fashion a flint into a cutting stone, he became conscious,
through trial and error, that only certain means of ac-
complishing the desired end were available. Thus he
could not reduce the rough stone to sharpness by hitting
it with a piece of wood. Wood, in other words, was not
a fit means to accomplish the end in view. Nor could he
do it by saying magical words to the stone. He had to
find another hard stone in order adequately to turn the
trick. In short, he learned that in this world, if one is
to get certain things accomplished, one must know what
things go together. Some things go together, some do
not.

Here was a dim sense that the world is not all a hodge-
podge. There are in it certain dependable relationships.
A hard stone can be depended upon to do certain things
under certain conditions. In other words, the world has
some recognizable structure to it. If one finds out the
structure, one can make use of it; if one remains in ignorance of the structure, one is helpless. The whole history of man as a tool-making and tool-using creature is

the history of his gradual discovery of more of the structure of the universe, more of the ways in which it hangs together. In all man's long period of emergence from savagedom, he went doggedly at it assuming that there was nothing really wrong with the universe, nothing that was fundamentally frustrating in it. The universe was there waiting to be discovered and, as it were, welcoming collaboration. The only thing that was wrong was himself. He was still too abysmally ignorant to know how to accommodate himself to the universe's ways.

The same persistent thought about an ordered structure and process of the universe was present even in man's shaping of religion. One of our distinguished scientists has made the mistake of believing that ancient man conceived of his gods as purely capricious beings that just happened to do the things they did without rhyme or reason. "The ancient world, in all the main body of its thinking, believed that God, or Nature, or the Universe, whichever term you prefer, was a being of caprice or whim." [4] And he compares this ancient way of thinking with the modern way. "Today, however, we think of a God who rules through law, or a Nature capable of being depended upon, or a Universe of consistency, of orderliness, and of the beauty that goes with order." This is hardly a fair statement of the case. It makes too sharp a break between ancient man and modern, and it loses sight of the fact that the impulse to believe in world-order and to act in terms of it is perhaps

[4] Robert A. Millikan, "What I Believe" (Forum, October, 1930, p. 196).

the most fundamental impulse there ever has been in man's life.

Primitive man, indeed, had curious gods and curious conceptions of what they did. But invariably those conceptions were based upon some sort of reason. It was not our more instructed reason, perhaps, but it was reason nevertheless. In a certain African tribe—which is a modern survival of the primitive—a child is brought to the medicine man. He discovers that the teeth have come in the wrong order. The child must be cast into the river. Why? The gods had arranged that teeth come in a certain sequence. Where that sequence is not followed, something is obviously wrong. The wrong must not be permitted to continue. Away, then, with the child. A pathetic mistake, yet exhibiting a dim kind of reasoning about the relations of things. In primitive times maidens were sacrificed to a god. The reason doubtless was a wholly erroneous one, but it was a reason nevertheless. Maidens were the means of fertility. To offer maidens to a god would bring fertility to the tribe. Again, pathetically mistaken, but nevertheless showing a dim kind of thought that there is an order in things, a connectedness, and that life can be successful only as it fits itself into that order and connectedness.

When we come forward to modern days, we discover a far clearer sense of what the cosmic order is. The sciences—mathematics, physics, chemistry, biology, psychology—have been progressively triumphant efforts to discover how matters hang together in the universe, what the basic connectedness really is.

The Principle of Coherence

Here, then, we discover something about ourselves, and thereby about our universe. We are creatures who inevitably act upon the assumption of an orderly universe. No one expects five times seven to change to forty-three over night. The sun may not rise tomorrow morning, but if it does not, it will be because something explainable has interfered with the solar processes. The universe which we inhabit, in short, is hospitable to logical thinking. Things in it hang together. As far as we know there are no really loose ends. If we found an apparent loose end, we should at once set to work to tie it in with the rest of the connected process.

We apparently learn something of significance through this. It is that one true way of life—true in the sense that it seems to match reality—is to find the relatedness of things. It is, in other words, to discover intrinsic coherence. Or, still more, it is to create coherence. To discover enduring coherence and to bring enduring coherence into life is, apparently, to move toward reality. For coherence—so the long history of man seems to have shown—can be acted out. It is only when we introduce an element into a situation that does not link up properly with the rest that conflict breaks out, and we go down in defeat.

So the matter stands, from elementary activities like shaping a tool or planting a field (we cannot plant a field with stones), to organizing a world state. Reality is relatedness. Our task is to discover that relatedness, or, where it still lies within the limbo of possibility, to bring it into being.

One Basic Quest

We discover, then, the reason for one of the most continuing quests in human nature—the quest for coherence, the movement away from the fragmentary and disconnected to the connected and the unified. The reason apparently lies in the fact that the universe is itself fundamentally a coherent system. We therefore do not succeed when we are out of harmony with the linkages of the real world. The fundamental process of life becomes one of connecting ourselves with the connectedness of the universe.

Here is one indispensable way of life. It is indispensable because everything depends upon it. We have to know what things fit properly together if we expect to be able to carry on life with any permanent success. The truth-seeker must submit himself without reservation to the realities, must in nowise manipulate the realities to suit his own ends. All this is necessary, we discover, since to manipulate the realities that exist in the larger universe to our own purposes and so bring together what does not belong together can, in the end, only mean disaster.

Truth, then, we find, is not only worth seeking, but must be sought for its own sake. That is why, in the present day, as the disinterested techniques of science become increasingly effective, there is a considerable turning away from the traditional religions as truth-systems. Religions apparently always have had an *arrière pensée.* They have wished the truth, indeed, but they have insisted upon having a special kind of truth, the truth that is satisfying to human beings. The disinterested attitude toward truth repudiates such a position. Truth must be sought even if the finding be fatal. For the truth-seeking process must be nothing more nor less than the entire submission of ourselves to what cosmic relationships really are. When, however, we thus submit ourselves we find that we become really free.

Here, then, we seem to find one dependable value in life. However else we may go wrong, we cannot possibly, at least in intent, go wrong if we hold ourselves rigorously to the search for truth. So Plato would seem to have the right of it. "In the heavens," that is, in the very constitution of the universe, there is the truth-principle. Truth is the first of the immortal three. To the best of our knowing that truth-principle is the principle of coherent linkage. We know only dimly as yet what the linkages are. Most of reality still remains an unfathomed mystery, but even for us, small human beings fumbling about in this nursery stage of our existence, it seems not impossible to say that in pursuing the way of truth we are pursuing the way of reality. If there is indeed defeat and disillusion, it is doubtless because, for some reason that lies within ourselves, untruth has become mixed up in the processes.

So it is patently false to say that in this world man lies under an inescapable sentence of defeat. For in pursuing truth, man has had his moments of triumph. Defeat there is, and nobility, happiness, and high endeavor still fare badly in the running. But if we place the blame for our defeat upon the whim of a creator, we seem to miss the most essential point of the matter, which is that there is something in the universe to discover and something which the universe, because it is apparently hospitable to logical thinking, permits us to discover. The challenge is really to our truth-seeking powers.

> "Horizon, reach out,
>   Catch at my hands, stretch me taut,
>   Rim of the world!
>   Widen my eyes by a thought." [5]

[5] Leonora Speyer, *Fiddler's Farewell*, p. 99.

Chapter XI

THE SECOND ELEMENTAL: BEAUTY

BEAUTY AS A LIFE-PRINCIPLE

LITTLE needs to be said in behalf of the second of the elementals. There is an incontestability about beauty which makes argument in its defence almost an impertinence. "I, too, will set my face to the wind and throw my handful of seed on high," cries Deirdre, in *Deirdre and the Sons of Usna*.[1] "For beauty is the most unforgettable thing in the world, and though of it a few perish, and the myriads die unknowing and uncaring, beneath it the nations of men move as beneath their pilgrim star. Therefore he who adds to the beauty of the world is of the sons of God. He who destroys or debases beauty is of the darkness, and shall have darkness for his reward.

"To live in beauty—which is to put into four words all the dream and spiritual effort of man."

One would have to go far indeed to find anyone so thoroughly consistent in his pessimism as to say no to the above. Beauty, by all of us, is accepted as an undeniable good; perhaps the most undeniable of all.

What, however, is beauty? The question should not be difficult to answer. And yet one suspects that beauty is like many another experience with which we are very

[1] Fiona Macleod (Mosher).

familiar. We know it so well that we hardly know it at all.

We call a woman beautiful, a child, a garment, a deed, a symphony. Let us suppose for a moment that each of these were not beautiful but ugly. What would we mean by applying such a term? Obviously the word would express a kind of aversion on our part. In the presence of the ugliness we should feel like drawing away. In this ugly woman, for example, we should find nothing which gave us a warm sense of wishing to approach, of desiring to remain as closely and as continuously as possible in her presence. The same would be true if the ugliness were in the child. We should wish the child removed. If the ugliness were in the music, we should stop our ears or desire to stop them.

Obviously, where there is ugliness, there is between the beholder and the object a sense of not rightly fitting together. There is a clash, a disharmony. Where, on the other hand, there is beauty, there is an instant sense of fitting together. This may be so strong that one is filled with a passionate desire to possess the beautiful object.

In order that there may be this feeling between beholder and object, there must be within the object itself a fittingness. If there is something in the object that "mars" the beauty, we mean by that that there is an element within it which does not belong with the rest. It is out of place. Thus music is beautiful to us when there is no dissonance that remains finally unresolved. A garment is beautiful when no line or color is discordant, a deed when no part of it goes counter to the essential

unity.[2] "Beauty," writes de Gourmont, "is a logic which
is perceived as a pleasure." [3] When we have said that,
however, are we not saying that the most fundamental
of all our desires is the desire for that integrated order
which is the opposite of irrelevancy, clash, conflict, confusion?

The Cosmic Basis

However much we may now smile at the simple He-
brew folk-talk of creation, there was in it a very real
insight. The first act of creation, according to that tale,
lay in bringing order out of chaos. When chaos was
banished and a world brought into being, the Creator
looked upon his handiwork with a joyous emotion and
pronounced it good. It was beautiful to him, because,
somehow, it fitted together.

The central and most unshakable insight of philosophers and scientists, poets, moralists and religionists tells
them that significant reality is order.

> "Order is a lovely thing;
> On disarray it lays its wing,
> Teaching simplicity to sing." [4]

Pythagoras caught the vision of it. Strumming his in-
struments, he noted that music is not helter-skelter, but
a phenomenon of measurable relationships. Every tone

---

[2] See an illuminating discussion of this in Wilkinson, Bonaro, *The
Poetic Way of Release*, Chap. XVI (Knopf).

[3] De Gourmont, Rémy, *Decadence*, p. 28 (Harcourt, Brace & Company).

[4] Anna Hempstead Branch, "The Monk in the Kitchen," *Rose of the
Wind and Other Poems*, p. 136 (Houghton, Mifflin).

is in mathematical relation to every other tone. Harmony is right mathematical relations; discord is wrong relations. He watched the movements of heavenly bodies. The planets moved in their orbits. They were related to each other with a precision that bespoke a cosmic regularity. He made a leap in thought and conceived the whole of reality as Number. The Number that is in music, he said, is the same Number that is in the heavens, in life, in human behavior, in everything. The universe is Number, and had human beings the power they might even hear the harmony of the spheres.

It was perhaps too swift a leap. A good deal of disharmony forces itself upon our attention, and we are less ready to ascribe a perfection of beauty to the universe. But the central idea still holds. Science approaches its ideal in the degree that it can express its data in number relationships. Science, in other words, makes the assumption that order is fundamental and that significance is achieved only as the world about us is seen in its measurable processes. Every atom is a computable process. Every flash of light is such, every drop of water or pressure of atmosphere.

For the scientist, the deepest wisdom lies in the pursuit of the order that is nature and in the adjustment to it and within it of our own life processes. If we are to do anything with atoms, or drops of water, or pressures of atmosphere, it is only in the degree that we discover the relationships involved.

For the scientist, as for the philosopher, these processes of nature have a profound and stirring beauty. The heav-

ens show forth an integration so far transcending anything of human fashioning that they lift our emotions
to another plane. The microscopic entities show niceties
of design that thrill us with their beauty.

Plato was caught up in like fashion. He saw a helter-
skelter world about him—the world of sense-impres-
sions: innumerable things unrelated, impermanent,
coming into existence and passing away, clashing with
each other—sights, sounds, emotions. But these things to
him were not the real world. The really significant world
was order. For him it was found in the great patterns.
Among all the diverse creatures that were men, he conceived that there was Man. Among all the diverse, more
or less imperfect efforts to achieve just judgment, there
was Justice. In the midst of all the more or less beautiful
things, there was Beauty. Above all and comprehending
all, there was the trinity of the Good, the True, and the
Beautiful. The Good was the True, and the True was
the Good. And always the Good and the True were the
Beautiful.

For Plato, as for Pythagoras, and for all the scientists
throughout history, the deepest reality was the beauty
that is order. And likewise for the moralist. For what is
goodness but the beauty of a fitting together in behavior?
To steal is to insert an incompatibility. It is to bring
disaffection, anger, bitterness, retaliation. To lie, kill,
be brutal, to be overweening in pride—all these are
confusion-breeding behaviors. They drive us back toward
chaos. Happiness, said Plato, is a harmony—within oneself and in relation to fellow-beings. When, later, Kant

laid down the rule that one should treat humanity, whether in oneself or in others, as an end and not simply as a means, he was indicating the same fundamental principle of a goodness that is at the same time a beauty. For to use a human being simply as a means to one's own ends is to arouse resentments. It is to pull life apart into dissentient opposites. It is to bring ugliness. On the other hand, to use each human being as an end in himself is to generate a functioning integration. The Good, therefore, in so far, is the Beautiful, because whatever is beautiful fits essentially together.

Beauty as a Triumph of Life

Here, then, we conclude something fundamental about reality. The least adequate form of existence— complete frustration—is chaos, confusion; the acme of existence is a perfect fitting together.

Within our human experience, beauty is a triumph, for wherever there is beauty, chaos has been banished, the impotence of confusion has been overcome, and a vital integration has been achieved.

That is why ugliness is a depressant. For the essential character of ugliness is to impede and diminish the life-process. The presence of ugliness, as we have seen, makes us shrink. We cannot go out to it joyously, identifying ourselves with it; we cannot continue our life out into it. "At the sight of ugliness she frowns and contracts and has a sense of pain and turns away and shrivels up, and not without a pang refrains from conception." [5]

[5] Plato, *Symposium.*

The Significance of the Arts

This will enable us to give a place of significance to certain creations of man that have not always been rightly estimated. In education we lay stress upon the practical tools of life—arithmetic, spelling, grammar, economics, language. These are essential, but it may be seriously questioned whether they are sufficient. No one of them gives the individual the peculiar emotion of a fitting together, a vital wholeness of existence (although a deeper study of them might induce this emotion). But in each of the fine arts this is precisely the kind of emotion we experience. Consider, for example, a symphony. In the first place, it has an integration which life, on the average, seldom achieves. It is not made up of irrelevant parts. It is not a miscellany of accidents. It moves with a fine unity of design and with a rhythmic flow that carries it on to its conclusion. This is precisely how we should like life itself to move. But life, on the average, is quite different. We are constantly being forced to adjust ourselves to irrelevancies. We try with difficulty to hold to the unity of the design, the rhythmic flow of our life, but the exigencies of existence have a way of breaking in upon that unity and rhythm.

Music, then, is *the way we should like life to be*. When we hear music—or create it—we are achieving unity of experience. We are for the moment living into a wholeness of design. This is why music can be a powerful civilizer. As we live successively into such unities, we grow the habit of experiencing the beauty of their integration.

Life emerges from its fragmentariness and frustration; it senses the beauty of a wholeness, which, in its everyday processes, it does not achieve.

Every fine art, in greater or less degree, has this effect upon us. A great piece of sculpture is the organization of matter out of relative formlessness into significant form. It is a unity that has no distracting irrelevancies, a whole that animates all its parts and in which all the parts together animate the whole. It gives us an experience which, in its rhythmic unity and faultless ordering of parts, is what we should like the rest of our life to be.

There is a real psychological importance in this. These arts—when we experience them—are not a mere idle addition to life. That is how they are frequently conceived. They are themselves *ways of life*. That is, when one hears music or stands before a noble structure, one is living just as truly as when one does the routine things that are necessary to one's existence. In truth, one is living in some of the most essential ways in which one can live. An individual might eschew all the arts, confining himself only to the needful things. What he would actually do, in that case, would be to fail to live in certain ways that are perhaps the most nearly perfect that human beings can achieve.

It is curious how persistently we regard the routine activities to be "life," while we regard listening to music or creating it, seeing pictures or painting them, listening to poetry or writing it, as experiences that are, somehow, a kind of irrelevant addendum to life. Take the example of the reading of a great novel. Let the reader select the last one that deeply stirred him. Let us say that he began it at eight o'clock at night and read absorbedly into the small hours of the morning. Suppose now that he compares this experience with the dictating of a number of routine letters in his office on the previous morning. Was the experience any less living? While he was dictating his batch of letters, he may have been interrupted a dozen times by telephone calls; several of his subordinates may have come in on one mission or another; he may have had some minutes of irritated search for a notation he had misplaced. A morning's work. That was "life." And now, at midnight he is at chapter eighteen. He scarcely knows what has been happening around him. He is far away from his room. He has been conversing for four hours with interesting people. He has been looking at their problems, following their eager expectancies, sympathizing with some of them, detesting others, watching the whole magic thing called life unroll itself before him.

At midnight has he really lived four hours of as vital life as he lived in the routine hours of his office? How does one measure this curious thing called life? According to our foolish conventions, this man was actually living when he was in his office, but only incidentally living when he was reading. Is not that a false valuation? *Life is what takes place in one.* The only question, therefore, is whether anything of transforming moment was taking place between eight in the evening and twelve o'clock midnight. And we know that that is what actually happens in such cases. Emotions are generated that are not usual in the routine hours, ideas and possibilities are opened that are normally closed.

That, one may suspect, is the essential truth in regard to all these ways of life which we call the fine arts. When we listen to a symphony or see a drama, we are living a life; when we read a poem which affects us deeply we are doing likewise. And by far the most significant fact is that in the music or drama or poem we are living life on the level of beauty—the level, that is, on which life becomes in profound measure a vital unity.

We might say, then, that beauty is as essential to life as anything that life needs. Without beauty we can indeed live—as animals or as mediocre human beings; but with beauty we enter into those triumphant integrations that are life at its highest.

Chapter XII

THE THIRD ELEMENTAL: THE GOOD

THE OBJECTIVITY OF THE GOOD

GOODNESS is not a word to conjure with today. The last thing we wish is to be "good." We wish rather to be free, frank, adventurous. We wish to be happy.

Our present rebellion against goodness is not difficult to understand. It is our reaction against a scheme of existence that has overstressed morality and left out of account two fundamental interests of life. In the first place, Christianity, as an institutionalized religion, has laid no stress upon the pursuit of truth. Indeed, for the most part, it has been suspicious of the truth-seeking process. The truth-seeker might overturn accepted beliefs. Thus institutionalized Christianity has in the main been the foe of truth-for-its-own-sake. It has denied the first of the Elementals.

It has also, in the main, been the foe of beauty-for-its-own-sake. Beauty has been regarded as too seductive for weak mortals. Beauty has a way of withdrawing the individual from a concern with his invisible soul to a concern with distractingly visible things that not only have nothing to do with his immortal spirit but frequently lead it to ruin. Christianity has not believed in this world.

162

It has believed rather in a salutary removal from this world and from all its fascinations. It has denied the second of the Elementals.

Thus institutionalized Christianity has left us hungry for two of the great sources of human satisfaction. It has stressed one point—love. There is indubitably a beauty and a truth in love. But as emphasized in institutionalized Christianity, love has been simply a form of morals.

Today we are rebelling against the moralistic view of life. We even lean over backwards and rebel against morality itself. What we wish now is truth. We ask for the right to be fearless about it, to be frank and open, to be skeptical even if our skepticism leads to the overthrow of everything we have ever believed. And we also wish beauty. Having been denied it, we wish it all the more ardently. We inveigh against the moralistic drabness of life. We more than half suspect that drabness and moralism somehow go together. At any rate we deny the right of any view to take from us that enduring fascination of beauty which seems to give life one of its major justifications.

So it is a little precarious to defend goodness. Perhaps if we confess at the outset that goodness without truth and beauty is never really goodness at all, we shall be permitted to continue. Goodness is a special kind of truth and beauty. It is truth and beauty in human behavior.

We are aware from our experience that human behavior may go well or ill. A great deal of it goes tragically ill. The newspapers are mostly accounts of how badly human behavior can fare. There is nothing particularly beautiful about stick-ups in dark alleys, or raping, or political lying, or the mutual slaughter of people. Nor is there anything particularly true about them. They are indeed both untrue and unbeautiful. By that we mean that they have no real place in the scheme of life. They help to defeat everything that we believe to be enduringly worth while.

There is nothing arbitrary about such condemnation. It is not simply that we do not *like* these things and that another order of human beings trained to other appreciations might positively like them and encourage their perpetuation. We know that they cannot belong in an enduring scheme of existence. Given full scope, they are self-defeating. They cannot be acted out completely and produce a consistently successful order of life.

This is important, for there has been a frequent tendency to believe that our judgments of right and wrong are subjective and therefore have nothing to do with the larger order of things. It was Huxley's belief that morals were, so to speak, man's invention. One discovers no trace of them in the physical or animal universe. In a sense this is true. One finds no Charity Organization Society among the barnyard fowls, and no rule of "women and children first" among the nautical beavers.

But we must doubtless go deeper in our thinking than this. A very slight examination seems to indicate that right and wrong are in a profound sense removed from our human choice. We cannot, for example, choose whether we shall make lying a recognized and honorable

social procedure or not. A society in which there could
be no mutual trust would inevitably go to pieces. In like
manner we cannot choose whether we shall have murder
as a permitted and approved mode of life. Where everyone is subject to murder at every moment and in every
circumstance, life simply cannot carry on its associated
enterprise of living.

These things are not subject to our choice. They are
beyond it. There is something in the process of existence
that compels us to recognize the laws of veracity and of
respect for life. We disregard these laws with the same
unfortunate results which we encounter when we disregard the law of gravitation.

In short, what is really "right" as between human
beings and what is really "wrong" are grounded in some
nature of things beyond our interference. Our frequent
unwillingness to subject ourselves to many of the supposed rules of right and wrong is a natural objection to
purely man-made rules, rules that do not seem to have
the imprimatur of a wider order of things. Thus when
women are told that it is not "right" for them to vote
or to go about without veils on their faces, the answer
is, "Who declares it is not right? Men? Then we shall
do these things." But if something beyond the choice of
man indicates that a thing is not right—as in the case
of lying or murder—we surrender to that which is more
authoritative than ourselves.

At the present time we are in two minds about the institution of monogamic marriage. There are those who
believe that a freer sex relationship should be permitted.

They refer to monogamy as a man-made institution. How is this issue to be decided? By show of hands? Obviously the matter goes deeper than that. We are really obligated to find out what scheme of sex relationship most widely and most lastingly works. This means that we are seeking to know the objective truth about sex behavior. We are, in short, interrogating nature.

Goodness is Truth

Thus the good life is not some moral scheme which we, in our timidities or our distrust of one another, have organized for the weariness of the flesh and the boredom of the spirit. Fundamentally, the good life is the life that achieves truth in behavior. It is the kind of life which will be permanently actable.

We have already analyzed cruelty as a way of life that involves its own defeat. Hate is likewise a self-defeating way of life. It pulls apart rather than unites. As long as individuals hate each other they have not found a mutually supporting way of existence. Acquisitiveness, when made the predominant motive, is likewise a self-defeating mode of existence. It impels one to draw things to oneself away from others. It thereby generates resentment. Apparently a healthy order of life cannot be based on the predominance of the acquisitive motive.[1]

The Principle of Integration

Psychologically speaking, unhealthy life is disinte-

[1] Tawney, R. H., *The Acquisitive Society, passim* (Harcourt, Brace & Company).

grated life. There is, for example, the multiple personality. The parts of the self do not hang together. One self splits off and goes it alone; then another and another. Perhaps they are all in jumbled conflict. One can never be sure of such an individual. He can never be sure of himself. He is a house divided and therefore lacks permanence and effectiveness. The problem of such an individual is, if possible, to get himself unified. Again, there is the insane person. He is one whose fantasies cannot be linked up with the world of reality. He is a little world in isolation. That world, in itself, may be a unified one, but it is futile, since it cannot relate itself to the larger world to which the individual belongs.

Health is integration, the parts linked in harmonious working relation. But so, in like manner, is truth always an integration. A binomial equation hangs together. Change any one of its parts and it falls to pieces and is algebraically worthless.

A truth-system, in short, as we noted in a previous chapter, is a coherence system. That is why we can say that certain ways of life are not true ways. War, for example, is an indication of a failure to find in human behavior the basic linkages between people. People destroy one another because they fear one another. They have not yet been able to find the basis of common interest. War apparently will disappear when human life discovers that the factors which link groups of individuals together are far more fundamental and delightful than those that keep them apart. The world-problem today is to develop common or unifying interests to such a point of indispensability that war will be simply unthinkable.

To say all this is to say that the human task is to create a cosmos among us, a world of effective order and relationships. This is perhaps an unintended way of complimenting the universe. For it recognizes the fact that human life can be fully successful only as it builds for itself the same harmonious interplay of relationships that seems to be characteristic of the larger universe.

The Fundamental Issue of Behavior

If, then, we take our cue from truth-systems, the chief objective of life would seem to be to establish behavior relations that are enduringly coherent. This is what the "good" life must mean. The defeats that we suffer—so easily set down to the whim of a creator—would seem to arise from the fact that we have scarcely as yet learned the most elementary facts about the coherence-possibilities of our life. In the first place, we have only just begun to become acquainted with the major linkages of the natural world. Obviously if we were more adequately acquainted with the laws and processes of the natural world, we should be able to lessen or even to eliminate the demoralizing effect of disease and thereby import an energy into life that is now almost beyond our imagination. Furthermore, if we knew better the laws, processes, and possibilities of our emotional life, we should be able to carry on, individually and collectively, with a greatness of productive harmony that is now beyond our conceiving.

The Fundamental Need

Human life, in brief, grows more adequate as it grows increasingly competent in the linking of itself with the various realities of its environment. If this is true, then the basic educaton of life should be a training in unification or integration. We subscribe to that in a way when we take the child, who, left to himself, would, as he reached maturity, run about seeking what he might devour and whom he might embrace, and put him into mathematics. The child is not at all pleased. This is not what his natural instincts call for. But in mathematics we relate him to the major verities of number and space. Again, we lead him out of his childish isolation into the major movements of history. We thereby seek to make him intelligently a part of the mankind to which he belongs. Also, we lead him forth from his only half-considered thoughts and half-understood emotions into the wider expanses of human thought and emotion. Through poetry, drama, the novel, the discoveries of the scientists and the reflections of the philosophers, we integrate his life with what superior minds have thought and felt.

So, in various ways, we make him into a creature linked in wider scope with his world. That unquestionably is the true course which education must take. We do it clumsily and ineffectively as yet, and it is for this reason, doubtless, that, after an average course of schooling, men can still do tragic things to each other, and women can still sentimentally bind up the wounds. But unsuccessful as we still are, the direction of life would seem clear. The way of truth is the way of fundamental integration. We achieve the thoroughly good life when we learn in all possible ways how to link our behaviors with reality around us in such measure that an enduring coherence results. Thus Truth and Beauty come together, on the human level, in the Good.

Part Four

THE PARADOXICAL QUEST

The mortal nature is seeking as far as possible to be everlasting and immortal.

PLATO: *Symposium*

Chapter XIII

BEYOND THE NARROWLY HUMAN

THE CORRELATION OF PLANES OF REALITY

ALL that we have said in the foregoing may be admitted. And yet, it might be objected, it signifies nothing as to the wider universe. It describes reality on the human level. It tells us nothing whatever of reality beyond our human type of experience.

"Here all is but a restless contention of shadows that pass presently; here all that is visible and all the colors known to men are shadows dimming the true colors, and time and death, the darkest shadows known to men, delude you with false seemings: for all such things as men hold incontestable, because they are apparent to sight and sense, are a weariful drifting of fogs that veil the world. . . ." [1]

Plato expressed the limiting subjectivity of our experience in a notable figure. We human beings are, as it were, like individuals chained in a cave. They face away from the cave's opening, their eyes turned toward the dark interior. Behind them is a high wall, and on the wall figures walk back and forth, talking among themselves. The light from the opening streams past these figures

[1] Cabell, James Branch, *Figures of Earth*, p. 125 (Robt. M. McBride & Co.).

173

and casts their shadows on to the dark interior. The chained individuals look at the shadows, and since they cannot turn around and see the living figures on the wall, nor the light streaming in, they believe that the shadows are the reality.

That was Plato's account of life: a self-deluding commerce with shadows.

More than Shadows?

Is that, however, the final word? One might suppose that an alert mind among Plato's cave-men would eventually note at least the synchronization of voices and shadows; and he might commune with himself: "No— it is quite true that we are fated always to see only shadows. But these shadows are not helter-skelter and haphazard. They come and they go in ways that seem to have some rhyme and reason." And we can conceive this superior individual setting himself to the task of noting the shadowy exits and entrances, and of plotting the correlations of voice and behavior.

In short, even shadows report something. Let us suppose—since metaphors are in order—that we are creatures bound irrevocably to the earth-plane. We are on a broad expanse of meadow. We can indeed look up, but we can never go up. There are the proverbial chains that bind us to the earth. Above us float clouds; and beyond the clouds shines the sun. Three planes, then—the earth-plane, the cloud-plane, and the sun-plane. We look down at the grass, and we see moving shadows. Now the shad-

ows thicken, now they diminish, now they disappear altogether. This may perplex us for a while—as long as we
merely keep looking at the grass. We may conjure up
divers curious explanations. We may decide, for example, that grass has a way of turning black sometimes;
then gray; then green. Or we may devise other explanations for these shifting phenomena. But if we do
differently; if when the blackness comes, we look up and
see a gray cloud; if when the blackness lightens, we look
up and see the gray cloud turn to a white one; and if
when the grayness turns to green, we look up and see no
cloud at all, we begin to get a dim sense of things somehow hanging together. We can, to be sure, since we are
earthbound, never know *what* those things above us are:
they are in another plane of being; nor what the shining
thing beyond them is: it, too, is in another plane of being.
But we can at least note the correlations. And noting
them, we can make out that the things that are happening on our earth-plane have some very real connection
with the things that are happening on the cloud- and
sun-planes.

This, of course, is only a metaphor, and must not be
taken too literally. But it may be suggestive of a certain
inevitable relation in which we stand to the larger order
of things.

Projections on Different Planes

Let us approach the idea from another angle. Instead
of taking earth-planes, cloud-planes, and sun-planes, let

us turn to dimensional planes in space. For example, let us take a three-dimensional figure, a cube. Let us select three points on the cube, one on each dimension. Obviously those three points will have a certain spacial relation to each other, as we find if we draw lines connecting them together. Suppose, now, that we project these three points on to a flat surface, a two-dimensional plane. The results will again be three points in a spacial relation—if connected, they might now form a triangle, or a straight line.

What is significant to note, now, is that while the relations of points on the two-dimensional plane are quite different from the relations of points on the three-dimensional plane, yet they are rigorously linked together. The two-dimensional relationship of points is *a two-dimensional way* of expressing the three-dimensional relationship, and conversely, the three-dimensional relationship is *a three-dimensional way* of expressing the two-dimensional relationship. The two-dimensional plane, we might say, manifests the relationship present on the three-dimensional plane.

Is this not an understandable relationship between ourselves and other possible higher orders of being? Apparently there is no complete disconnection between ourselves and these higher orders. It is true that we, as human beings, are strictly limited by all the limitations that are human. We have only a few senses, crude and inaccurate at the best. We have a mind that is perhaps only partly developed and that thinks in terms of its peculiarly limited concepts. To suppose that with this meager equipment of ours we are able to compass the absolute of reality is of course the sheerest nonsense. And yet it is not inconceivable that that reality which far transcends our human comprehension manifests itself, in a way, on our human level. To disbelieve that, indeed, requires a much harder belief, the belief that there is a complete disconnectedness of reality. It requires that we seriously hold the view that this small human circle of happenings is like an island in the universe, absolutely cut off from all the rest of what is real. That is hard to hold because it goes counter to the most impregnable of our beliefs, the belief, namely, in the connectedness of reality.

Correlations

The poet-philosopher, Tagore, expresses something of this relationship in words that might otherwise seem vague and mystical: "Entering my heart unbidden even as one of the common crowd, unknown to me, my king, thou didst press the signet of eternity upon many a fleeting moment." [2] He would seem to mean that in the small commonplaces of human experience there is something that adumbrates the wider and more enduring reality.

Shelley has used another metaphor to express our relationship to the greater reality:

> "Life, like a dome of many-colored glass,
> Stains the white radiance of Eternity."

While the colors and the patterns on the human plane

[2] *Gitanjali*, p. 35 (Macmillan).

are not the white light and the patterns of the "eternal" plane, there is a correlation between them.

Graven on Our Surfaces

The Hindu poet-philosopher has expressed the same thought in another way: "These ancient seers felt in the secure depths of their minds that the same energy which vibrates and passes into the endless forms of the world manifests itself in our inner being as consciousness." [3] This may readily be misunderstood—as it frequently has been. It may be taken to mean that because the most essential reality about us is our consciousness, the universe or the absolute is consciousness. That was the ill-considered conclusion which certain idealists in philosophy seemed to reach. Tagore does not make his seers say that, and we, doubtless, should not say it. What they say tells nothing of what the cosmic reality itself is. It simply asserts that, whatever it is, it *manifests itself* in our inner being as consciousness.

Our conscious life, in short, is, as it were, one of reality's cross-sections. There is reality below it and above it. It is incapable of going out of itself to either, but, inevitably, the lines graven on its surfaces are projections of all the reality there is in the world.

This leaves us, to be sure, with an agnosticism about our world. But not with a hopeless agnosticism. For it assumes that what we find to be significant on this par-

---

[3] Tagore, Rabindranath, *Sādhanā*, p. 21 (Macmillan).

ticular plane or cross-section of reality has a relation to significances beyond itself.

Tantalus

Such a view begins to make many things clear. Above all, it makes clear the ceaseless hunger of man for the infinite, his endless quest after that which, apparently, he can never compass. He hungers for beauty, and when he finds it, it crumbles to dust in his hands. It was not the radiant thing he thought of in his dreams. He hungers for the consummate truth, and when he comes upon his small fragments of wisdom, they seem so utterly inadequate that he is tempted to give up in despair. He hungers for a glory and a majesty of life, and when he compasses his small achievements, he finds that they are but caricatures of the greatness which he seeks. And yet he goes on hungering. He is the everlasting Tantalus: the Real is always just beyond him, and apparently it always will be.

If, however, it is as we have conjectured, this endless defeat of life becomes life's one way of endless triumph. On his human plane man is inevitably shut out from the realization of significances that are beyond him. But there is on his plane the teasing reminder of these. They are, on his level, the projection of reality that is beyond that level. Man, then, is apparently at his highest as he responds to this reminder, as he seeks what he never can quite compass. It is in this—everlastingly fraught though it may be with defeat—that the essential drive of his life lies. For despite all the ultimate frustrations, he goes on turning his defeats into new desires and new determinations.

The Universe and Ourselves

So we come back to our question about the universe and ourselves. We can frankly admit that in its fulness the universe is beyond our knowing. We can, in short, be agnostic. But we seem to have the right to believe that if we find what is significant on our human plane, we thereby discover something that has a significance beyond the merely human.

"The mortal nature"—to quote Plato once more—"is seeking as far as possible to be everlasting and immortal." It fails, repeatedly fails, will always fail. When, however, we understand why it fails, we are saved from the pessimism that so largely prevails where life is seen simply at close range as a wretched series of humanly confined and humanly generated wishes, blunders, poltrooneries, and illusions. When human life is seen as a cross-section of the life of the universe, a cross-section on which are projected significances beyond itself, we can understand the agonies of its joys and the triumphs of its defeats.

Chapter XIV

LOVE AND THE WORLDLY WISE

A MODERN EVALUATION

L OVE has come upon dark days. It used to be regarded as the goal of all our questing, the consummate type of human experience. Through love the
dull mortal was supposed to be transformed into something very like a god. All that was in the tradition. But
now? Between biology, clinical psychology, the erotic
novel, and the realistic scandal-sheets, love has come
forth a bedraggled figure.

Love as a Disease

As a disease, love is variously described. It is shown
(with the tongue in the cheek) to be a malady that has its
regular time of onset, its period of incubation, its characteristic symptoms of feverishness and of mental and
emotional unbalance, and its gradual subsidence into
normal health. Every one of us is subject to the malady,
as no effective methods of immunization have yet been
discovered. So we can all jest about our common ailment.
In fact, for the most part, it is a pleasant ailment, albeit
making us a little foolish, and, at times, eventuating in
embarrassing complications. To watch others while under

the disability of the disease is to realize its ludicrous character.

Then there is a more serious manner of description. Love is a disease the onset of which is incomprehensible and the effects of which are frequently devastating. Suffering from its graver forms, individuals do what under normal circumstances they would not dream of doing. They are gripped by a power from which they vainly struggle to escape. It is as if some poison had entered their systems, overturning their minds, making them mad with a madness they partly know but are impotent to cure. An instance of such a description is found in Somerset Maugham's *Of Human Bondage.* One recalls the almost incredible infatuation of Philip for the waitress, Mildred. Even while he is passionately following her about, he hates her and detests her, but he cannot escape from his degrading enslavement. The novelist is not chuckling. He is profoundly serious—and bewildered. What is this monstrous compulsion, he asks, that makes wreckage even of the best? What is this insanity in life? He sees no beauty in it. He sees in it only a form of human bondage.

Nature the Deceiver

Again, there is the view that love is one of nature's neat tricks. Nature has important work to do. In order to get it done she must put burdens upon us. Of ourselves and in our sane moments, we should not undertake those burdens. They run variously from suffering agonizing pains in childbirth to clipping the wings of ambition and settling down to making provision for home and provender. Nature is apparently too subtle and too wise directly to bid us do these things, so she casts over us a veil of illusion. She makes the commonplace appear rare beyond comparison; she changes the features of ordinary individuals so that they shine like the faces of gods and goddesses; she transforms prosaic acts into noble gestures and invests everyday contacts with an allure of ecstatic loveliness.

She tricks us well. When it is all over, we recognize what she has done, but it is then too late. Nature retires, smiling, and we carry on her work.

Enter the Clinician

To complete the disillusionment comes the clinical psychologist. Love, to him, is no thing of considered choice; it has nothing in it of the divine; it is simply a furious urge within us. Do what we may, we cannot escape it. It lurks in the hidden recesses of our being, driving us in childhood to curiously disturbing and anti-conventional behavior, in adolescence filling our minds with a phantasmagoria of unmentionable images, in maturity, and even in old age, obsessing us with desires that sometimes end in tragic outer complications or in almost equally tragic inner conflicts. It invades not only our waking but our sleeping life. In slumber it slips past the censor of our reasonable hours and induces us to act out fantastically its feverish and ofttimes inhuman wishes.

This love is a tyrant that ramps through our life seeking whom and what it may devour. At the best we can only keep the tyrannous thing in momentary restraint. In incredible ways, it breaks through our best defenses; it turns wise creatures into foolish, gentle creatures into cruel, occupied individuals into individuals endlessly and hopelessly distracted by a fever that they both ardently desire and bitterly detest.

The Fourth View

One suspects that every intelligent person today has come under the influence of one or the other of these views, probably under all three. Thus, after the centuries that have been spent in hymning it, love comes out a rather sorry figure. The belief in romantic love seems to be one of those passing episodes of unbalance in the life of the race that eventually runs its course, to be succeeded by something more nearly approaching realistic sanity.

So it is with hesitation that one ventures even to describe a fourth view, for in that view love is raised to very great heights. In fear of overwhelming waves of ridicule, one clutches at some floating object. In this case, perhaps, the best that one can find is Plato. For despite the passing of time and our own increasing sophistication, we still have a fondness for Plato, particularly when he speaks in the character of his beloved Socrates. With a little condescension, we continue to be willing to listen to him, even though we may deny to him that more authenticated view of reality which our modern age seems to have achieved. Perhaps this is because Plato was an artist. He could say things with rare beauty, and even though most of what he says is a little like moon-madness, we like the sound of it. . . . So we clutch at Plato.

Plato Speaks

" 'And now I will ask about Love: Is Love of something or of nothing?' [1]

" 'Of something, surely,' Agathon replied . . .

" 'And does he possess, or does he not possess, that which he loves and desires?'

" 'Probably not, I should say.' . . .

" 'Would he who is great desire to be great, or he who is strong desire to be strong?'

" 'That would be inconsistent with our previous admission.'

" 'True. For he who is anything cannot wish to be that which he is.'

" 'Very true.' . . .

" 'And the admission has already been made that Love is of something which a man wants and has not?'

" 'True,' he said.

" 'Then Love wants and has not beauty?'

" 'Certainly,' he replied."

We Turn to a Modern

There may be an idea in this brief dialogue which is worth considering. Wherever there is love, says Plato,

[1] *Symposium.*

there is a lack. There is a wish for something. Where there is no lack, there can be no love.

The logic would seem to be unanswerable, and we may turn from Plato for a moment to note how happily it fits in with much that is being written today about love. Indeed Plato seems to be giving us ground for our disillusionment. There is, for example, the notable erosoph, Cabell. The burden of his writing appears to be Platonic: to love there must be desire for that which one does not possess; once, however, one comes into possession, the desire ceases, and there is an end of love.

" 'Look you, adorable and all masterful Sesphra, I have followed noble loves. I aspired to the Unattainable Princess, and thereafter to the Unattainable Queen of a race that is more fine and potent than our race, and afterwards I would have no less a love than an unattainable angel in paradise. Hah, I must be fit mate for that which is above me, was my crying in the old days, and such were the indomitable desires that one by one have made my living wonderful with dear bewitchments.

" 'The devil of it was that these proud aims did not stay unattained! Instead, I was cursed by getting my will, and always my reward was nothing marvellous and rare, but that quite ordinary creature of earth, a human woman. And always in some gripping dawn I have turned with abhorrence from myself and from the sated folly that had hankered for such prizes, which, when possessed, showed as not wonderful in anything,

and which possession left likeable enough, but stripped
of dear bewitchments.

" 'No, Sesphra, no: men are so made that they must
desire to mate with some woman or another, and they are
furthermore so made that to mate with a woman does not
content their desire. And in this gaming there is no gain,
because the end of loving, for everybody except those
lucky persons whose love is not requited, must always
be a sick disgust and a self-despising, which the wives
will conduct in silence, and not talk about as I am talking
now under your dear bewitchment.'

"Then Sesphra smiled a little, saying, 'And yet, poor
Manuel, there is, they tell me, no more uxorious husband anywhere.'

" 'I am used to her,' Manuel replied forlornly, 'and
I suppose that if she were taken away from me again I
would again be attempting to fetch her back. And I do
not like to hurt the poor foolish heart of her by going
against her foolish notions; and, besides, I am a little
afraid of her, because she is always able to make me un-
comfortable. And above all, of course, the hero of a
famous love affair, such as ours has become, with those
damned poets everywhere making rhymes about my
fidelity and devotion, has to preserve appearances. So I
get through each day, somehow, by never listening at-
tentively to the interminable things she tells me about.
But I often wonder, as I am sure all husbands wonder,
why heaven ever made a creature so tedious and so un-
reasonably dull of wit and opinionated. And when I

think that for the rest of time this creature is to be my companion, I usually go out and kill somebody. Then I come back, because she knows the way I like my toast.' " [2]

It is a forlorn enough picture, albeit with a wry twist to its humor. Love reaches out for angels in paradise and awakens to find within its embrace drab figures of earth. One recalls the myth of Psyche. The love god was wise in his day. He must, he said—and he said it most particularly—remain unseen. And there was happiness for both of the lovers, while nightly they lay together shrouded in dark mystery. Poor Psyche! She had not read the Cabellian stories of disillusionment; for, eager to know her beloved utterly, she lit the lamp. The unattainable became the attained. And the love god vanished.

Plato Again

To all of which Plato would nod in sage understanding: "Love wants and has not beauty." To which the foregoing writer would add, "Precisely, and when love possesses what it has passionately wanted, then farewell both to beauty and to love."

But Plato might lift a considering eye. "Are you perhaps talking rightly of love or of some lesser thing that sometimes unaccountably is given love's name?" "Love indeed desires something," he might go on to say; "but

---

[2] Cabell, James Branch, *Figures of Earth*, p. 255 (Robt. M. McBride & Co.).

what really does love desire? Are you quite sure of that? Is it to possess something? Is it to hold something forever for itself? But, as you have truly observed, when love possesses, it ceases to desire, and so ceases to love.

"And yet there is something strange about that. Would love, do you think, desire its own extinction? It would then be a silly kind of process, hardly becoming a power that seems to have its moments of greatness. Let me recall to you what was said to Socrates by my wise old friend, Diotima. He asked her once what the object was which they who love had in view. And in her cryptic way she answered: 'The object which they have in view is birth in beauty, whether of body or soul.'

" 'I do not understand you,' he said; 'the oracle requires an explanation.'

Diotima Explains

" 'I will make my meaning clearer,' she replied. 'I mean to say that all men are bringing to the birth in their bodies and in their souls. There is a certain age at which human nature is desirous of procreation—procreation which must be in beauty and not in deformity; and this procreation is the union of man and woman, and is a divine thing; for conception and generation are an immortal principle in the mortal creature. . . . For love, Socrates, is not as you imagine, the love of the beautiful only.'

" 'What then?'

" 'The love of generation and of birth in beauty.'

" 'But why of generation?'

" 'Because to the mortal creature, generation is a sort of eternity and immortality,' she replied. . . . 'Wherefore love is of immortality. . . .

Different Kinds of Love

" 'Those who are pregnant in the body only, betake themselves to women and beget children—this is the character of their love. . . . But souls which are pregnant . . . conceive that which is proper for the soul to conceive or contain. . . . And such creatures are poets and all artists who are deserving the name of inventor. . . . He who in youth has the seed of these implanted in him and is himself inspired, when he comes to maturity desires to create and generate. He wanders about seeking beauty, that he may beget offspring—for in deformity he will beget nothing. . . . Above all, when he finds the fair and noble and well-nurtured soul, he embraces the two in one person. . . . And at the touch of the beautiful he brings forth that which he had conceived long before . . . and they are married by a far nearer tie and have a closer friendship than those who beget mortal children, for the children who are their common offspring are fairer and more immortal. . . .

" 'These are the lesser mysteries of love, into which even you, Socrates, may enter; to the great and more hidden ones which are the crown of these. . . . I know not whether you will be able to attain. But I will do my utmost, and do you follow if you can.

The Ladder of Love

" 'For he who would proceed aright in this matter should begin in youth to visit beautiful forms; and first . . . to love one such form only—out of that he should create fair thoughts; and soon he will of himself per- ceive that the beauty of one form is akin to the beauty of another; and then if beauty of form in general is his pursuit, how foolish would it be not to recognize that the beauty in every form is one and the same. . . . In the next stage he will consider that the beauty of the mind is more honorable than the beauty of the outward form . . . until he is led to contemplate and see the beauty of institutions and laws, and to understand that the beauty of them all is of one family. . . . And after laws and institutions, he will go on to the sciences, that he may see their beauty. . . . Drawing toward and contem- plating the vast sea of beauty, he will create many fair and noble thoughts and notions in boundless love of wis- dom; until on that shore he grows and waxes strong, and at last the vision is revealed to him of a single science, which is the science of beauty everywhere. . . .

" 'He who from these ascending under the influence of true love, begins to perceive such beauty is not far from the end. And the true order of going, or being led by another, to the things of love, is to begin from the beauties of earth and mount upwards for the sake of that other beauty . . . until he arrives at the notion of ab- solute beauty and at last knows what the essence of beauty is. . . .'

" 'This, my dear Socrates,' said the stranger of Mantineia, 'is the life above all others which man should live, in the contemplation of beauty absolute. . . . In that communion only, beholding beauty with the eye of the mind, he will be enabled to bring forth, not images of beauty, but reality. . . . Would that be an ignoble life?' "

The Creative Principle in Man

Disregarding the details, are there not perhaps two ideas in the foregoing that will bear consideration?

The first is that man, when one regards his most essential nature, is a creating or generating being. This is, as it were, the mortal in him that strives for immortality, "because generation always leaves behind a new existence in the place of the old." What man, in his fervor of love, desires, then, is not a possession—something to secure and to hold—but rather something, through passionate union with which, he may bring forth in beauty.

This may yield us a fair clue to the difficulty in which those characters—Cabellian and otherwise—find themselves in whom love, once it is consummated, turns to a sour taste in the mouth. If one follows their various careers, one notes that the love episode is always a preliminary, not to an ecstasy of creative life, but rather to a condition of temporary pleasure in the possession of the beautiful beloved. These characters, one and all, after the victory, do nothing more than live through a brief period of delight in the attainment, and then find that the experience palls.

If Plato is right about the essentially creative nature of man, there is every reason why they should find the after-experience palling. Something far more insistent and fundamental is present in these sex-saturated creatures. Not recognizing what this is, however, they attribute the boredom to the inevitable disillusion that must come with all achieved love—and then take what small comfort they can by seeking new bewitchments.

Granting that there is truth, however, in what Plato suggests, the whole matter might be open to a quite different interpretation. If love, in its real nature, is indeed a desire for begetting, a desire that can be consummated only by union with a beloved who can make the begetting possible, then the test of the love is not the temporary pleasure of possession, but the begetting.

In Plato's day, such a union between a man and a woman could, save in rare cases, be thought of only on the level of physical procreation. Any other kind of union was reserved for men, for women were confined to unintellectual pursuits and were therefore no fit mates for men of mind. But today matters are obviously different. It is frequently the men who are not fit mates for women of noble mind. Where, however, the really great thing happens, where there is, between a man and a woman, a marriage of minds as well as a marriage of bodies, is it not conceivable that the creative life of such a pair may well be a continuing delight?

This, it would seem, is all the more possible because in this kind of love—and perhaps in this kind only—the beloved, whether the man or the woman, continues to remain forever the unattainable. For the beloved is the source of begetting. As the source of begetting, the beloved is an indispensability and an endless fascination.

The Universal in the Particular

Plato's second idea also warrants consideration. The life-process, on any level of significance whatever, is, he indicates, a questing for that which is beyond any particular gratification or combination of gratifications. The achieved particular never completely satisfies. There is something in the nature of us which pushes us beyond the achieved or the experienced to the still unachieved and unexperienced. This, says Plato, is the dim working of the universal in us. From one beautiful thing we pass to another and another, until, at last, we emerge to a different level of experience altogether—we behold a beauty that runs through all things. We behold it in thoughts and institutions, in laws and behaviors. When we emerge to this level, we are no longer the simple, thing-minded individuals who take a naïve kind of pleasure in this, that, and the other. Things and individuals are then no longer opaque, separate things and individuals. We see *through* the particulars to the beauty of the reality which informs and illuminates them.

A modern writer makes one of his characters say: "I worship you, as I never knew that I could worship any

human being. I adore you because in adoring you I am
adoring the great life-possibilities that have always left
me breathless with reverence."

Is that a wholly impossible thought?

Quandary

It is hard in these days to decide. In the Cabellian tale
from which we have quoted, the beautiful Queen Frey-
dis, who was once a goddess and who could inform dead
images with life, herself came to her death at the hands
of the satirists. That may yet be the fate of love. The
fourth view which we have described seems, indeed,
outmoded. A little wearily and a little whimsically we
regard this queer excitement of men. And whether we
are to apply to it a clinical thermometer, or psycho-
analysis, or a shrug of the shoulders, we are not quite
sure. . . .

But still there is Plato. He is ancient, and yet, sometimes, he seems to be looking back at us from a future
of incredible loveliness.

Chapter XV

HEARTENING FALSEHOODS

THE REALITY OF POSSIBILITY

"Their heads haloed with immortal illusion." [1]

THIS discussion as to whether love is an illusion or
a reality leads us to a far deeper question about
life. Is life truly, as Plato would believe, a search for
reality? We have, on the one hand, those deeply serious
individuals, the scientists. No one would doubt that, in
their own opinion, they are searching for reality. And
yet one might make out an excellent case for the thesis
that they are in full tilt after an illusion. Thus, for example, they believe that the truth they find will really
matter, and in that belief they go ahead soberly, adding
up their increments of discovery. But then will come a
wind out of the universe and sweep all their increments
into the void. Civilizations have come and gone. Man
himself, it might be suggested, will doubtless himself
go, and the negligible ball he inhabits will be dispersed
as dust throughout the heavens, or gathered again into
other negligible balls where negligible fungus growths
will again mount their way to a transient protoplasmic
pride.

[1] Arthur Davison Ficke, *Selected Poems*, p. 173 (Doran).

Somehow that seems the soberer fact, but it is a fact which is not permitted to obtrude. These devoted workers keep up the energy of their effort because of a great hope, which might be said to be no real hope at all but an illusion.

And yet there would seem to be no more excellent way out. Better a dish of illusion, one might say, and a hearty appetite for life, than a feast of reality and indigestion therewith. William James coined the phrase "the will to believe." Such a will to believe, he said, is necessary if the nerve of action is not to be utterly paralyzed. In short, he seemed to imply, it is far less important what we believe than that what we believe should keep us stout of heart.

Even Plato, in spite of his passion for truth, was not averse to the conviction that life must in large measure be lived under the stimulus of lies. He made an exception in favor of his wise ones. But for the mass of individuals there must be heartening deceptions. The mass of people, as he knew, would, even in his ideal republic, have a fairly poor time of it. They must therefore be told some "needful falsehoods" lest they despair or grow ugly. They must be made to believe that however low and humdrum their place in life might be, they were framed by God for the special tasks which they were now performing. Let them be proud of the divine origin of their tasks and perform them for the sake of God and the common mother, their country.

This same attitude has not been altogether unknown in modern days. Until various sharp-eyed men of a more realistic turn saw through the pleasant sham, it was a prevalent habit to praise workers as the salt of the earth and to quote Scripture to them about the virtue of industry and the priceless things that spring from a hand that turneth not from its appointed task. In those days the simple workers, thus bedazzled, would fling up their caps and cheer lustily in honor of their own greatness and glory.

There are those who believe that religion all through the ages has simply been an exemplification of this pleasant habit of making life tolerable by needful falsehoods. It did not require designing priests to invent the falsehoods. As Voltaire might say, if there were not a falsehood ready to hand, each generation would itself have invented one. Or, as the Cabellian hero, Dom Manuel, had it on his shield: *Mundus vult decipi.*

Man wishes to be deceived because he needs to be deceived. Life, apparently, is too full of ugliness and inevitable defeat to be borne without drawing over its face a veil of illusion. Thus, it is pointed out, man liked to believe that gods listened to him up in the skies. It lessened his feeling of inferiority. It made him go more vigorously at the ferocious lower creatures, and it enabled him to build his mud hovels and bring forth his brood with some sense of its being dignified business. When he swung from trees he apparently had no need of gods. His imagination could not prevision the death that was awaiting him in yonder glade, nor could it make him anxious about the future of his babes. He was mercifully blessed with no mind to speak of. He was a delightful chattering fool with no need of great notions about himself.

But he lost his tail and gained a mind, and thereafter things were different. As our contemporary, Alfred Adler, might say, out of his inferiority he had to contrive a superiority. And he did it apparently by cleverly lying to himself about himself. Naked, shivering, beaten upon by a thousand fears, with the poorest physical adjustment to his environment of all the animal creation, he had to start whistling in the dark. And as he whistled the fancies came. He was Man, was he not? A pretty considerable fellow was Man. Anyone could see that great things were intended for him. Afraid of these prowling beasts? Hah! Were they not lower than he? Did they have any Friends up there? Tomorrow he would take out his flinted stick and show them!

So courage grew, and he learned to talk familiarly with his fancies. After a while, apparently, he forgot that they were fancies—if he ever knew it—and took it for granted that great things had been ordained for him in a world which, while it might have its unpleasantnesses, was not so difficult after all. If he was reminded of death, the destroyer, he smiled and pointed upward. It was all well with him, he said. And if it was indicated to him that things were pretty mean and ugly around him, he again pointed upward. In fact, through his process of needful self-deception—so the thought runs—he made himself invincible to logical attack. No truth could pierce the defensive wall of his beloved falsehoods. And so, invulnerable to the verity of things, he lived happily. For he had discovered the secret: "Better a good lie than a poor truth."

Living "As If"

A philosopher [2] has named this tendency in man with an appropriate name. This, he writes, is man's perpetual philosophy of the "as if." Man lives not *as* reality dictates, but *as if* reality were such and so. It is the addition of the "if" that is man's unique invention. Do we not find this to be true? Man lives *as if* (*als ob*) he were the chosen of God on earth, *as if* his gods were carefully lending him attentive ears, *as if* death were not a miserable ending to a succession of fairly miserable doings, *as if* he had a destiny resplendent and far-reaching. When he builds his states, he acts *as if* his king were of divine origin, or later, *as if* all men were really born free and equal and the voice of the people were the voice of God. When his chivalric heart swells within him, he acts *as if* ladies were delectable creatures of innocence that needed to be guarded against the mischances of mere mortality. When he falls in love, he acts *as if* the beloved had been ordained especially for him, *as if* his marriage were made in heaven. When he goes to law, he acts *as if* twelve jurymen selected from those of his fellow-citizens who read nothing and know nothing and have no opinions upon anything were suddenly transformed into Solomons of wisdom and justice. And when he goes into business, he acts *as if*, in transferring unimportant things from one

[2] Hans Vaihinger, *Philosophie des Als Ob.* English edition, *The Philosophy of "As If"* (Harcourt, Brace & Company).

group of unimportant folk to another, he is doing something of real significance.

It is all very perplexing for those of us who have been brought up on the stern commandment: "Thou shalt not lie." Apparently man has wrought for himself a far more pleasing commandment: "In all ways that enhance thy happiness, thou shalt bear false witness."

Romance

Man heartens himself on the romantic lie. The hero with the square jaw and handsome eyes and the habit of doing incredible things that no world of reality ever witnessed, is the hero he loves to watch. He can sit through hours of beholding him at his impossible feats and never once say "Fiddlesticks!" He likes the lie. It seems to do him good. Or if, once in a blue moon, he finds someone who does say "Fiddlesticks!" he discovers this to be a sour young person with internal troubles. The healthy, hearty, normal male—the male who, as we say, does the work of the world and is the backbone of the nation—loves the romantic lie. The truth would leave him not only bored but disgusted.

All through his known history, man has fed himself on romantic lies. The exploits even of his flesh and blood heroes have always been exaggerated, and he has not only swallowed the exaggeration but thriven on it. Indeed, he has never felt quite right until he has made his conquering heroes into something very like gods. Then he could swarm out with his neighbors, gaping at his heroes as they passed in their golden chariots. Curiously enough he never felt small or demeaned by witnessing these impossibly noble creatures. They were himself—at least they were what he would have been if circumstances of birth, and the rest, had not ordered things differently. That was exactly the swagger he would have affected, exactly the haughty lift of brow and glance of lion eyes!

He has done the same thing with the exploits of his saints. He has always exaggerated them beyond conscience. Apparently he had to believe them to be such workers of miracles as never had appeared on earth. He could respect such as they. He could yield them his credulous soul and be happy in the yielding. For somehow, his unmiraculous and shabby life needed this assurance of a more than earthly power. He thereby drew power to himself. He went away from gazing at his pious fabrications with soul uplifted and heart aflame with happy devotion.

The romance of all his romances has been woman. All through the ages, out of his dreams and his yearnings, he has built his incomparable Helen. To be sure, she was always only a lady of his dreams. The lady he actually embraced was a spindly, spotted Joan or an overfleshed and painted Susan. But he stuck to his Helen. If he could not bring her home to his mud house on the hill or to his cottage in the suburbs, he could at least live with her in that gorgeous palace of his imagination with an ecstasy no church-made union ever permitted.

Is Man Merely Self-Deceived?

And so the story runs. What shall we make of it? Is man indeed a curiously self-deceived creature? Is he the dupe of his own imaginings?

It has been said that man does all this because reality, being as futile and generally uninteresting as it is, needs to be escaped. Man's only way of escape is into a region of lies. But if that is true, then man is not really the dupe, but rather an astute fellow who has learned how to circumvent a world of reality that is far too mean for his resplendent imagination.

Schopenhauer expressed this need of escape. Reality being an endless striving that is either dissatisfaction or boredom, man should turn to art as his way of escape. More recently, Bertrand Russell, in his *Free Man's Worship*, has voiced a similar view. Reality, in an ultimate sense, he has said, has nothing to offer us. The world of life and man is doomed to an utter extinction. Man's only hope, then, is to invent a world of his own. Out of his imaginings, he can build glories that reality has never compassed. It is for man to make an acceptable life for himself in that artful region of his own contriving.

Indeed the word that one most frequently hears on the lips of these disillusioned ones—disillusioned, be it noted, as to *reality*, not disillusioned as to the value of illusions—is "escape." The chief business of life is an escape from a reality incapable of yielding what the high heart of man desires. There may be truth in this, and the thought warrants examination. However, it is worth recalling that the word "escape" may be followed by one of two prepositions: there may be escape *from*, and escape *into*.

What Are Illusions?

Let us examine these illusions of man somewhat more particularly. Might not a good case be made out for the thesis that an illusion (of the kind we have been describing) is not a falsehood but rather a special and, indeed, important kind of truth?

A book has just been published containing the memoirs of Kiki, the girl who queened it in the bohemian quarter of Paris. The New York *Times* reviewer, in commenting on the book, writes: [3] "Kiki grew up with no particular background of schooling, to go to work very young and to get on in life by means of her physical self and her personality. She was shrewd because she had no particular illusions and could live life realistically as so much pure experience; she was naïve because she had no sense of values, no gift of objective penetration." "Shrewd because she had no particular illusions." If we hear that said about a person, what is our reaction? Are we not a little disquieted, put on our guard? We do not like people who are thus cold-bloodedly shrewd. We have a feeling that at a pinch they will use us. We sense a kind of hard keenness that can well be solicitous for Number 1, but that, under pressure of need, will be for-

[3] September 28, 1930.

getful of Number 2. Indeed that seems to be the ethics of the Montparnasses of the world.

Perhaps we are maligning Kiki, for she was and still is a prime favorite. Let us, however, take up this question of illusions. Recall the illusions we have been describing—the hero-illusions, saint-illusions, woman-illusions. Recall the illusions that parents are under in regard to their children, patriots in regard to their country, religionists in regard to their heaven-ordained function and destiny. Would it be untrue to say that in each of these cases the illusioned person refuses to accept what is before his eyes as the complete reality? The parent, for example, has a squawky, ill-mannered child. You and I look at the child and accept the fact of its present squawkiness and bad manners. We are realists. We see what we see. But the parent, apparently, sees more. He sees possibilities; at least he ardently hopes there are possibilities. In other words, he sees what the child has it in him to be. When he loves the child, therefore, and yields the vigor of his life for the child's upbringing, is it this present squawky child to which he devotes himself, or is it the child in all the dimly conceived range of his possibilities?

The realist is right. The child is squawky. But the illusioned parent likewise is right. The child may some day cease to be the disagreeable creature it now is. The question is who is most right; and the answer seems obvious.

Our illusions, in short, from this point of view, indicate that we refuse to be confined to present facts.

Possibilities as Realities

All art, is, indeed, an escape. It is an escape from immediate, factual, this-minute reality. It is an escape from confinement to a small, literal, present perception of life. It is an escape *from*. But is it not also an escape *into*?

Shall we say that it is an escape into *unreality*? That is a prevalent expression among the disillusioned. It is a correct expression if we are willing to call possibilities unrealities. But it would seem to be nearer the truth to call possibilities a special and important kind of reality. Thus the possibilities that lie in an individual are not by any means unreal. They are perhaps the most real thing there is about him. Take away all his possibilities, and he is reduced to the momentary bundle of flesh that instantly becomes dead matter. Grant him the possibilities, and a living process is ahead of him.

Possibilities, in short, are realities. Perhaps, indeed, they are the most important realities. If so, then the type of mind which disregards possibilities and holds itself rigorously to the present facts is a profoundly untrue kind of mind. Art seems to be significant because it refuses to be thus realistic. It escapes from life into the greater possibilities that life has within it.

Commerce with the More Potent

So man, all through the ages, has built for himself and in behalf of himself his world of illusions. Has it been altogether a world of lies? To the literal-minded, yes. There were no gods in the skies, listening to the prayers of those primitive creatures. And so, literally, we must say that primitive man deceived himself. But is this a sufficient account of the matter? Does it go deeply enough into the psychology of our nature?

"For there is that in every human being which demands commerce with something more fine and potent than itself." [4] May not this be the clue? The human creature, apparently, is not an automaton that smoothly does what it is appointed to do. He is rather a mortal mind reaching out to something more than its present rather mean mortality. Man's religions, pathetically foolish and misinformed as they have been, would seem then to have been but a projecting upon the screen of the universe of the greater possibilities which man has felt within himself. He was not merely this dirty, foody, warmth-seeking, sex-craving animal. He had a kind of godness within him. He had powers that some day would companion with the divine. Give him time.

Doubtless it has been this drive toward a kind of suspected greatness in himself that has made man the advancing creature he has been. Was it a lie that urged him on? Or was it the half-conscious perception of the reality of his own inherent possibilities?

We know that his childish imaginings went through maturing processes. They did not remain forever as naïvely fantastic as they were in the first years of his life. Centuries of contact with realities sobered him, broadened his view of things, gave him a surer sense of what was

[4] Cabell, James Branch, *Beyond Life*, p. 81 (Modern Library).

worth believing. In that whole maturing process, however, he never lost touch with the basic part of his belief.
Stubbornly, despite all appearances to the contrary, he
held on to the belief that there was something greater
than himself and that there was something greater *in*
himself.

So he has gone on fashioning new gods and new conceptions of his own relations to his new gods. Doubtless
the process is far from ended. Today he is seriously reviewing that celestial world of his imagining which he
built for himself some two thousand years ago. There is
much in it that now displeases him. The celestial heroes
are no longer to his liking. They do not represent *him*.
So, half-unconsciously, he is shaping a new world for
himself. Again, as always, it will be a thing of his imagining. It will go beyond any truth that he can factually
authenticate. But it will be the world of his greater
dreams. It will be the reminder to him of something
that he will never be quite able to compass, but that he
will always—since he is man—go on trying to compass.

The Truth of Man's Romancing

And so with all the rest of man's romancing. It has,
indeed, been foolish and immature and sentimental and
naïve. But all of it, whatever the misconceptions, has
revealed his stubborn holding to a basic fact. Kings may
not be divine, but they ought to be, and perhaps might
be. Men may not be born free and equal, but they ought
to be; and some day, if we are wise enough about it,

they yet may be. The voice of the people may not be the voice of God, but somewhere hidden away in them is something of what we like to call divinity. Men may not be the heroes we make them out to be, but we know that, inadequate as they are, that is what they would wish to be and some day may be. Women may not be the breath-taking creatures we believe them to be, but there is in them a divine allure that we shall seek endlessly, because, fleshed over with mortality though it be, we know somehow that it is there.

Illusion, then, of the kind we have been describing, is man's faith in his unrealized self. It is his faith and his power. Take it from him, and he returns to the brute. Let him refine it and exalt it, and he goes his way toward what is greater than himself.

Chapter XVI

SEEKING A PRINCIPLE OF BEHAVIOR

BEYOND ETHICAL CONFUSION

AS moderns, we think naturally and easily in terms of laws of nature. Primitive man, on the other hand, thought in terms of gods, demons, nymphs, storm-spirits, and similar creatures. A large part of his technique of life consisted, therefore, of various rites devised for the purpose of persuading these beings to do what he wished them to do. To the degree, however, that these persuasion-rites had no causal connection with the physical phenomena—a chanted prayer, for example, had no relation to the success or failure of a crop—primitive life moved ahead disappointingly. No great advances were made until this attitude was abandoned and the physical world was conceived as orderly processes subject to discoverable laws.

In the physical realm the victory of law over animistic inexplicability is fairly won. As a result, we are now convinced that to discover the laws which prevail in the multiplicity of happenings is the surest way to gain understanding of them and such measure of control as lies within our power. This, we conceive, is the function of the physical scientist, one which we expect to see fulfilled increasingly well.

The Psychological Lag

Meanwhile the psychological realm lags behind. We are only just emerging from the period when the psychological life, like the physical, was supposed to be in the control of beings who needed to be placated and persuaded. Doubtless this is why the psychological—including the ethical—life has thus far advanced so disappointingly. For our techniques of persuasion have, in the main, had little to do with the objective phenomena. For a ruler to make sacrifices to the gods in order to insure victory on the battlefield obviously had less to do with the reality than the training of an army. For the anxious sinner to perform ceremonies in order to avert the anger of the gods was of far lesser moment than vigorously to build new habits. For an individual out of employment to pray for help had less connection with the actual situation than to improve himself at his trade or to induce his fellows to organize that trade more equitably.

We Seek an Alibi

Much of our despair about human life arises out of the retention of the primitive view that life is governed by mysterious beings beyond our understanding and control. The Russian dramatist, Andreiev, opens his sardonic *Life of Man* with the figure of "The Being in Gray," the spokesman for an inexplicable Power—stern, unyielding, reasonless—that rules our fate. We are mere puppets in its hands, and as puppets we pass through all the senseless cycle from a childbirth excruciating to the mother to tragic old age and death. And yet, as one reads this drama, one sees that the tragedy, as often as not, lies not in some Power beyond, but in the character of man himself. The first act opens with the agonies of a mother giving birth to a child. The implied thought is: "How horribly this God that rules all inflicts suffering on mothers." And yet a moment's reflection makes it clear that human mothers suffer only as long as medical and hygienic ignorance prevail. The play proceeds to describe the distress of the architect who can find no adequate reward for his talents. But obviously for that tragedy no reasonless Power is to blame, but simply human ignorance of how to organize the economic order. The drama, in brief, supposedly an indictment of the Power that rules us, is really an indictment of ourselves.

One may say the same of Cabell's sprightly comedy, *Jurgen.* It never seems to occur to the clever Jurgen as he makes his amorous way through life, searching after justice, and as he comes in the end to believe that life is either the jest of a whimsical creator, or a pathetic irrelevancy issuing from a creator too busy to notice, that the essence of the continual defeat lies in the character of Jurgen himself and of all his associates. One looks in vain throughout the book for one individual that is really admirable. All of Jurgen's love-making proceeds on a plane little higher than his animal impulses, and those to whom he makes love are in little better state than himself. Jurgen, indeed, despite his pretentious flourishings, does not confront life. He simply has no conception of life's possibilities. His tragedy, like that of all his fellows, is the tragedy of psychological ignorance and under-development.

When We Accept the Challenge

It is curious to note how pertinaciously we cling to this primitive way of regarding our life as governed by uncontrollable fates at the same time that we have completely emancipated ourselves from such thinking when it comes to matters of the physical world. We do not, for example, moan about our fate when, having built a bridge, we find that it collapses. We go over our mathematics to discover where we fell short of complying with the mathematical and mechanical laws of nature. But nevertheless, when our psychological life comes to all manner of sorrow and defeat, we write in melancholy fashion of the implacable fates that rule our ways.

All this, indeed, is in the long human tradition. The Greeks conceived of Zeus as a tyrant and Prometheus as a suffering rebel. The Hebrews thought of God as the tester of man, and Job as one who, through all his inexplicable suffering, still retained his faith in the inscrutable dispenser of his fate. In the English morality play, *Everyman*, we have the pointed lesson that only through the grace of God, the sacrifice of Christ, the intercession of Mary, and the offices and sacraments of the priesthood, may *Everyman* be saved. In the mediaeval legend of Doctor Faustus, we have the Good Angel trying to persuade Faustus to discontinue his scientific researches and to rest in unquestioning faith upon the vision, grace, and mercy of God. "Sweet Faustus, think of heaven and heavenly things."

It is this animistic tradition which has held us back from a rigorous inquiry into the laws that govern psychological and ethical life. If, however, we know that physical mishaps occur when there is ignorance of physical laws, it would seem justifiable to conclude that when psychological mishaps occur, it is doubtless because there is ignorance or misapplication of the basic requirements of psychological life. Wisdom would then seem to demand that we search out the laws of the psychological and ethical life as thoroughly as we have searched out the laws of the physical world, in full confidence that when we discover them life will be brought far more widely and effectively within our control.

Milton describes Samson as refusing to lay the blame for his misfortunes on heaven:

"Appoint not heavenly disposition, father.
Nothing of all these evils hath befallen me
But justly; I myself have brought them on;
Sole author I, sole cause." [1]

These lines mark the transition to what may be regarded as the modern point of view. Our human evils are, in the main, humanly caused. And they are so caused

[1] *Samson Agonistes.*

not because of any original malevolence in ourselves, but chiefly because we are in ignorance about ourselves. We are, in short, in much the same condition in respect to our mental and emotional life as was the primitive in respect to the physical world. The chief need, therefore, is to gain as penetrating an understanding of our human behaviors as we have already gained of the behaviors of atoms and protoplasmic cells.

What is apparently necessary is to discover, if we can, a principle or law of the ethical life that is as fundamental and far-reaching, let us say, as the law of falling bodies in the physical world.

Is there such? The answer will best be found by analyzing typical defeats and successes in human life.

Considering Business

Let us first consider the economic process. It is notably one in which there is a large amount of defeat and suffering, a large amount of ugly triumph and ill-gotten success, and a small amount of noble achievement.

We now begin to see that there is no inherent inevitability about the evil in the process. We increasingly realize that business and industry have for many centuries operated on a false principle, namely, that of gaining for oneself through the loss of others. Thus the merchant who could sell an inferior or defective article at an unfair price was supposed to be the successful type of merchant. Business was a process in which the buyer had to beware, and the seller had to be expert in the ways of deceit (*caveat emptor*). Again, the employer who could bully men into working for the lowest possible wage was supposed to be the really successful employer. It was expected of him as a matter of course that he would coerce his workmen into accepting what he was willing to offer, as it was likewise expected of his employees that they, if they were powerful enough, would coerce him into giving them what they desired.

If we ask why business and industry have been ugly, the answer seems clear: the principle of business operation has been supposed to be that of mutual oppression. In the present day, however, we are discovering that such a supposed principle is actually self-defeating, that it is not the true principle of business at all, but only a result of quite unenlightened thinking.

A merchant seems to acquire a better understanding when he realizes that his best asset is satisfied customers. He must not deceive them; he must not ask of them exorbitant prices. Paradoxically enough, he must do the most he can for *them*. When he realizes this, as we now begin to perceive, he builds up a successful business. He and his customers alike prosper.

An employer begins to have a more adequate understanding when he realizes that his best asset is satisfied workers. He must not oppress them; he must not pay them wages which make them sullen with anger. He, too, paradoxically enough, must do the best he can for *them*. He must voluntarily give them the highest wage consistent with the industry's output and the best working conditions within his power. When he does this, he builds up an industrial organization that is alert, resourceful, and coöperative.

Business life, then, succeeds in the degree that it makes it possible for other lives to succeed. It seems possible to say that it never enduringly succeeds on the basis of making other lives less prosperous or happy.

Considering the Family

We may carry these considerations into other human relationships. A prevailing view of marriage was that it was one of male domination. The wife, for the most part, was an individual suppressed, curtailed in her opportunities, kept within narrow limits of housewifery and childbearing, or regarded as a mere sexual partner. The man himself, though apparently triumphing, was actually defeated. For under such conditions, he lived with an individual who could give him no such response as would aid his own individuality to further growth. The older view of marriage, in short, based itself upon an ethical error identical with the one we found prevailing in the older forms of business and industry.

The more modern view of marriage, on the contrary, bases itself upon what seems to be a clearer ethical insight. It is the view that a true marriage is one in which each member aids the other to the unfolding of potentialities. In such a marriage, the husband gains as the wife gains, and the wife as the husband.

We know, too, that parents who oppress their children, or use them for their own ends are, in general, laying up for themselves an old age of sorrow and disappointment, whereas parents who regard the welfare of their children as one of their major obligations provide for themselves, generally speaking, an old age of precious satisfaction. Parents, in short, gain as their children gain. But likewise children gain as their parents gain, for the children of parents who stop short in their growth-processes lose as inevitably as their parents lose.

Considering Political Relationships

The same considerations apply in the relations of a government to its people. The French monarchy tyrannized over its people and reaped a whirlwind in the Revolution. The Russian czardom for a like reason went down to deserved disaster. Similar considerations apply to governments in their relations to one another. The customary relation has been one of enmity. Each nation has regarded itself as a self-sufficient, sovereign entity, potentially or actually surrounded by foes. To conquer and subdue have been the chief national aims. All this, as we well know, has led the world into disasters for which no superhuman fates are to blame. Only man's ignorance of the effective relationships of peoples has been responsible.

The Ethical Principle

The foregoing will doubtless be sufficient to reveal that for which we have been searching. The fundamental principle of ethical life, it would seem, might be expressed as follows: He succeeds who makes it possible for others to succeed. We might call it the principle of ethical polarity.

If we pass in review all the behaviors that bring various disasters to humanity, it would seem clear that each of them does so because it fails to take account of this principle. Thus, if we consider the Seven Deadly Sins, we find that each of them is, in one manner or another, a disregarding of this principle. Pride is the first of them. It is an overstressing of oneself, a dwelling upon oneself to the exclusion of others; it is the refusal to let others be of equal moment with oneself. Covetousness is the second. Obviously it again is an overstressing of the self, with the added error that it seeks to draw all to itself even at the cost of the unhappiness of others. Wrath is the third. Wrath is an obsession of rightness on one's own side, and a failure to see rightness on the other side. Envy is the fourth. It is hatred of the happiness of others; it is the wish that they be less happy so that one may oneself be more happy. Gluttony is the fifth. The unwisdom of gluttony is obvious. It is a gorging of oneself in such measure that one destroys powers that one might fruitfully employ; and it is usually a greedy unconcern about what others receive. Sloth is the sixth. In a world where energy is reciprocal and polar, sloth is a refusal to make the appropriate return effort. It is the wish to take things to oneself effortlessly, to reap without sowing. The seventh is lechery. It is the use of others for one's sexual pleasure without regard to their own well being.

Thus the Seven Deadly Sins are simply seven ways of disregarding the fundamental principle of polarity.

The Error of Self-Sacrifice

This principle was expressed by a master of psychological and ethical insight when he said that he that loseth his life shall find it. Unfortunately this expression of the principle has been misinterpreted to mean that the true way of life is the way of self-sacrifice. Self-sacrifice is never a true way of life. It is often disastrous in its consequences. The mother who sacrifices herself for her children too often sacrifices her children, inasmuch as she tends to make them into selfish creatures. Thus in losing her life in the sacrificial way, she not only loses her own life, but theirs as well.

Individual life, to be healthy, must give as well as take, take as well as give. As in the physical world there can be no positive pole without a negative, so in the psychological realm there can be no enduring success for oneself that does not involve enduring success for others.

The Human Tragedy

These things seem so clear that one hesitates even to say this much about them. And yet a cursory glance over the history of mankind shows that the chief attitudes of men have been a direct contradiction of this fundamental principle of behavior. Take any score of outstanding historic events—wars, conquests, dynastic successions, exploitations, tyrannies—and the basic motive in practically all of them is found to fall either under one of the Seven Deadly Sins or under some other form of wishing to gain through the loss of others. When the inevitable consequences have come, it has been customary to attribute the ill results to everything except the simple fact that the true psychological way of life was missed.

It was, as we know, after the discovery and formulation of the law of falling bodies that the remarkable advances were made which brought the physical world so largely within our control. Is it unreasonable to suppose that when with equal clarity this fundamental principle of polarity is grasped there will be notable advances in our organization of human relationships? Where the principle is now recognized, there already are found incontestable results. In family life, the application of the principle that he succeeds who makes it possible for others to succeed is developing a far more fruitful relation between husband and wife, parents and children. In the economic world, it is bringing a realization of a more satisfactory relation between employers and employees. In the world of politics—most backward of all—it is developing a consciousness that nations must eventually beat their swords into ploughshares and live together with mutual respect and aid.

When we have said all this are we not finding once more what we discovered early in this discussion, that the authentic trend of life is toward the development of increasingly significant wholes? For in the relation of reciprocal enrichment, in whatever sphere of life it may be, there is accomplished a wider and more enduring integration. But the integration is of a kind that is never complete. Thus, again, we are apprized of the paradoxical nature of our human quest: what we seek is always being achieved and yet forever remains unachieved.

Chapter XVII

THE HEROISM OF UNCOMMON SENSE

A DOUBT ABOUT PESSIMISM

"They went forth to battle but they always fell.
　Their might was not the might of lifted spears.
　Over the battle-clamor came a spell
Of troubling music, and they fought not well.
　Their wreaths are willows and their tribute, tears.
　Their names are old sad stories in men's ears.
　Yet they will scatter the red hordes of Hell,
Who went to battle forth and always fell." [1]

WHEN we think of supreme greatness, we are apt, most often, not to think of victorious achievement but rather of defeat. We think of Socrates drinking the hemlock, of Christ on the cross, of Giordano Bruno burning at the stake, of the Christian martyrs awaiting their fate in the arena.

We may interpret these happenings in various ways. We can keep our eyes fixed upon the suffering of these men and upon the stupidity and cruelty of a mankind that causes the suffering. Then we draw the inference that life, for the most part, is a thing of hopelessness and self-frustration. Or we can keep our eyes upon the

---

[1] Shaemas O'Sheel, "They Went Forth to Battle," *Jealous of Dead Leaves*, p. 12 (Boni & Liveright).

dauntless willingness to suffer. Then we disregard the thousandfold banality of life and detect in the courage which faces defeat that impulsion toward the as yet un-achieved which would seem to give human life its su-preme quality.

Much of our contemporary literature is apparently taking the first course. It is seeing man in his smallness, meanness and unrelieved futility. There is good reason for this. In the past, the literary artist was in large measure a spokesman for the optimists. That virtue is always in the end triumphant and vice defeated, that the course of true love never runs smooth, but that, given time and circumstance, it reaches its appointed happy goal, these were the axioms on which the major proportion of fictional art was built—from Sunday-school stories to best sellers. The modern novelist re-volts against the dishonesty. As a consequence he is at present going to the opposite extreme and emphasizing everything that points to the drab self-defeat of virtue, the triumph of vice, and the relative absence of any-thing that can be called true love. He deliberately ban-ishes the nobly heroic from his novels.

To an extent this is salutary. A little viciously, per-haps, but with honest intent, he is laying the old senti-mentalities to rest. When he has completed his task and begins again to look at life, he will have prepared us for a juster evaluation. It may be that then a new type of literature will develop which will—with precisely the same honesty—fix its eyes upon man, not at his mean-est, but at his noblest. And it will doubtless find him at his noblest as, in the spirit of the foregoing stanza, he goes forth to battle, to fall.

As the contemporary pessimists miss the reality of the type of heroism which our poem describes, so do the contemporary success-philosophers. They seem not to have learned that life may be too great to be successful, that their kind of success can be purchased only by shutting the eyes to the distant and grasping what is near. Worldly wisdom would indeed seem to dictate the latter course. No doubt all the above mentioned men were, in this sense, stupid men: Socrates was stupid, so was Christ, and so was Giordano Bruno. A good, sensible, biologically conceived philosophy of adjusting oneself to one's environment would have bidden these men be more sensible.

Examples

Values, in these matters, become curiously inverted. Among those whom we account great, stupidity may be wisdom. I count as the most enduring of my own experiences contact with a few men and women who have been too great to be successful. One of them was Joseph Worcester. I remember his quiet work with discharged prisoners. When the day of their release came, and they were sent into a world that drew its skirts away from them, he would take them to the discarded street-car that he had converted into a room on the ocean shore and give them a home in which to live. Then he would go about among his friends and seek work for them. A discharged prisoner, he knew, has little chance for honorable occupation. He secured work for his men, guarded them against the blackmailers who were forever on the trail of the ex-convict, helped them with his own counsel and confidence. Sometimes he failed. His men went back on him. The struggle was too hard for them, and they drifted again into the easier way of crime. Sometimes he succeeded. But from the point of view of what we normally call success, Joseph Worcester was a failure. He built no notable institution, devised no over-mastering new way of life.

Another was George Holmes Howison, a great teacher of philosophy. Reared for the ministry, he found the ministry enslaved by a crude and fanatical religion. Entering the life of philosophy, he found philosophy capitulating to a crassly conceived materialistic science. He shattered his lance against both. Out on the western edge of American civilization, he brought down upon his head the anger of the little men of the pulpit who were then powerful. One would suppose that he might have found support in the men of science. But, speaking for the dignity of the mind, he was met by the indulgent smiles of those for whom the mind had become but a passing incident in an evolutionary scheme of things that was meaningless and without direction. He was an ardent spirit, a really great man, and though he had his band of devoted followers, he went down in eventual defeat. Even the world of philosophy, that is now beginning to move in the direction in which he moved, scarcely knows him.

Another was a senator from Belgium—Henri La Fontaine. When the war was at its hottest, and even the Christian churches had placed a moratorium on Christ, La Fontaine was using every ounce of his energy to build up a world commonwealth. He came to America with the belief that America would listen and take effective steps to bring about a saner order among men. He lectured to more or less apathetic audiences. A few were fired, but as for the millions, the new fashion in life was saving democracy by shooting the befuddled clerks and teachers and school-boys who were the enemy.

Other men eventually took up the work of La Fontaine, and, with half his vision, produced that pathetic and yet poignantly wistful hybrid, The League of Nations based on the Versailles treaty. I saw La Fontaine in Geneva once. He was still worlds ahead of the petty national politics out of which even the League could not seem to extricate itself. He was still tilting for the impossible. And I suspect that practical politicians looked upon him indulgently, suffered his talk—and then went about the more important business of protecting their national honor.

I need not tell of Jane Addams. I suppose the war was to her the most heart-breaking experience in all her life. Jane Addams was the outstanding woman of America. She is no longer, in the popular sense of that word, the outstanding woman. She is a pacifist, and that is enough to condemn her in the eyes of those who, with an incredible persistency, carry on the lusts and hates of an older heritage. She would gladly have joined the Debses and Chaplins in prison if a notorious officialdom had dared to place her there.

Nor is there need to speak at length of Margaret Sanger. Notwithstanding that we make earnest protestations about our wish for a more decent world, she is still regarded as one who, in her efforts to achieve that more human decency, is herself committing an indecency. Curious topsy-turviness of our thinking! She makes a plea for pity—for the unwanted children that come into homes too meager to give them welcome, for the devitalized women and their bewildered mates. And we ask the police to escort her to prison.

What Our Admiration Implies

In such individuals as these we seem to find life on its most significant level. This is attested by the fact that we eventually give their heroism of uncommon sense our profoundest admiration. Each generation, to be sure, has a way of misunderstanding and martyrizing its great ones, but succeeding generations awaken to the tragic blunder and lift the despised and rejected into places of honor.

We may easily wax ironic over the constant repetition of this apparently stupid process of yielding praise to greatness when it is too late. But the process itself has its significance. On our average level of life it is difficult to evaluate what is beyond the average level. Let us suppose that I know very little about music, that I am, in short, an ordinary person habituated to the ordinary musical appreciations. How shall I know, for example, whether Scriabin, who assails my ears with unfamiliar sounds, is a musical genius or a musical charlatan? Because the sounds are unfamiliar, I shall probably not like them. Am I to be greatly blamed if I assert that they are not music?

The great ones among us are great precisely because their insights and loyalties are beyond the average. The ordinary Athenian could not comprehend that queer fellow, Socrates, who insisted upon pestering everybody with embarrassing questions. Why did he not stick to his work, make a decent living for his Xantippe, and leave respectable folk to go undisturbed about their business? They could not see that Socrates was loyal to a new kind of loyalty. Today that new kind of loyalty is both understood and respected. Every true scientist is a Socrates who spends his life putting questions to the stubborn realities that he confronts. We honor Socrates today because we are now able to see that what he perceived as the true way of life is the true way of life.

In short, we have moved up to Socrates. It is in that *moving up* that the significance of this whole process of martyrizing our great ones and then honoring them lies. They are, as it were, the spiritual magnets of the race. They draw us up to their level.

When we examine their own lives we note that a like process takes place in them. Average life moves about on a fairly fixed level of interests. It moves, but, so to speak, horizontally. The life, on the other hand, of the individuals we have been considering, is drawn upward from the average level of interests by the powerful attraction of something that is above that level.

If we admire these individuals, it is doubtless because we recognize, even though unconsciously, that the true destiny of a human being lies in identifying himself with a reality that is beyond the achieved and accepted.

Our highest admirations, then, would seem to indicate that the veritable way of life is not the way of mere adaptation to environment. That is a biological description which is quite inadequate for human life. It halts us at the static virtues of decorum and respectability. The true way is rather one of projecting oneself into a yet unrealized order of values. When that is done, present existence is placed in a larger setting. It achieves the dignity of a more comprehensive understanding. And in the light of the greater values thus revealed, it becomes a powerful source of mounting life.

"Vain is the chiming of forgotten bells
    That the wind sways above a ruined shrine.
Vainer his voice in whom no longer dwells
    Hunger that craves immortal Bread and Wine.

"Light songs we breathe that perish with our breath
    Out of our lips that have not kissed the rod.
They shall not live who have not tasted death.
    They only sing who are struck dumb by God." [2]

[2] Joyce Kilmer, *Poets* (in Joyce Kilmer, *Poems, Essays and Letters*, George H. Doran Company).

Part Five

IN THE LARGER SETTING

*This secret spoke Life herself unto me: "Behold,"
said she, "I am that which must ever surpass itself."*
NIETZSCHE: *Thus Spake Zarathustra*

Chapter XVIII

OUR EMERGING LIFE

THE DIRECTION OF HUMAN DEVELOPMENT

EVOLUTION, we believe, is an ongoing process. But if so, then development that is of evolutionary moment must be proceeding within ourselves. We ask, therefore, what the direction is in which we are going. Scientists have asked themselves the question, but for the most part they have confined their interest to two aspects of our life: physical structure and social institutions. They measure the shapes of our skulls, plot the curves of their development, and seek to predict what manner of craniums will later come to be. Or they plot the growth of institutions—property, marriage, government—and seek, by casting back into their past, to cast forward into their probable future.

Practically no attention, however, has been paid to a far more fundamental aspect of ourselves, to that aspect, indeed, which might be said to be a chief creative agency of our future, namely, our consciousness. Our present form of consciousness has been taken for granted as a kind of invariant—like the invariant of light. It has been taken to be what it is, and no one seems to be asking whether it is not itself even now undergoing significant development.

A Venture into the Future

In the year 1901, a remarkable book was published by a Canadian physician and psychiatrist of wide reading and penetrative originality.[1] Of that book, William James, always the eager pioneer, wrote: "My total reaction on your book, my dear sir, is that it is an addition to psychology of first rate importance, and that you are a benefactor of us all." Speaking of the form of conscious life which Bucke conceived as the next stage to be achieved in human evolution—as, indeed, already being achieved among us—James continued: "Let me say that you have brought this kind of consciousness 'home' to the attention of human nature in a way so definite and unescapable that it will be impossible henceforward to overlook it, or ignore it, or pooh-pooh it entirely away."

And yet it is significant to note that in the thirty years since Bucke published his remarkable work, practically nothing has been done in the investigation of the idea which he suggested.

Nevertheless this idea is so obviously important that it would seem to merit instant attention. It is the idea that, inasmuch as evolution of life-forms (including the psychological) continues, we have every reason to believe that a further form of our conscious life is already observable among us—in high degree among certain

[1] Richard Maurice Bucke, *Cosmic Consciousness.* (Dutton and Company).

rare individuals, in lesser degree among most of us. The full emergence into that further form, Bucke suggested, would naturally not be instantaneous—the whole of humanity leaping, so to speak, into a new order of being. As in all the stages of evolution, we should expect a slight difference in one more happily circumstanced individual, then in a few others, then in more, until finally the new form would become widespread and secure. What he proposed was that we look about to see whether there are any outstanding examples among us of a form of conscious life which might properly be regarded as of a higher order than that with which we are familiar. This, he suspected, would not be a form totally discontinuous with our normal consciousness, but one which would already be adumbrated in the more significant processes of our mental and emotional life.

In his book Bucke asks us to recall the fact that man's particular form of conscious life did not exist on this earth for many millions of years. It was a relatively late emergent, having been preceded by the earlier stages of mere sensitivity and mere perception. But when it finally came to its fulness—self-consciousness—the ability to know oneself as a self over against the not-self—it was momentous in its effect. It made language possible; it made possible an apparatus of conceptual thought which opened the world to exploration and control; it made a moral order possible—devotion, sympathy, the sense of right and wrong.

It is not inconceivable, Bucke writes, that when man

emerges fully—as he is now emerging partially—into his next order of conscious life, the effect will be of profound moment.

Searching for Examples

The significant aspect of Bucke's book is his search for conspicuous examples that present this process with a clarity not found in our average life. He might, indeed, have simply theorized about the question and done nothing more. Plotting the curve of our past forms of conscious life, he might, with a good deal of plausibility, have theoretically cast forward into the future. But what we know of emergent evolution warns us against such a procedure. The new emergent, we seem to find, is not predictable from the old orders. Hence no amount of theorizing about the direction which conscious life, judging from the past, would *seem* to be taking, would be safe. Nature, apparently, has a way of springing surprises. We must, therefore, not seek to prophesy about nature; we must go to nature for the facts.

His book is a going to nature for the facts (nature in the more inclusive sense in which we have used the word). In this case, the facts are not examples of lower orders of existence, but examples of an apparently higher order. He examines those individuals, in short, who have had a peculiarly outstanding effect upon mankind.

They are persons who, for the most part, have been chiefly a puzzle to us and in most cases to themselves. Jesus was so much of a puzzle that he was deemed di-

vine. Buddha was a similar puzzle and was raised to
divine status. Paul's sudden and dramatic transformation, which was the beginning of a career of notable
power, was likewise regarded as of more than earthly
origin. Mohammed, a great regenerator of his people,
was worshipped as a prophet of God. Socrates spoke of
himself with perplexity. When it came to the deepest
matters, he said, it was not he himself that spoke, but
some "daimon," or "voice" within him. Plotinus, the
Alexandrian mystic, a man of noblest character, revered
by all who knew him, and of superb mentality, felt that
his insight had come through a passing out of the ordinary condition of consciousness into one of what he
called *ecstasis*. In that condition he saw as ordinary eyes
do not see, felt as ordinary feeling does not feel. He
experienced a transfiguring oneness with the source of
all. Swedenborg, another man of unquestionable greatness, albeit a madman to those who did not understand
him, felt that he saw with a spiritual sight the things
that to the carnal eye are hidden. Balzac, the Shakespeare of the *Comédie humaine*, speaks of a highest kind
of seeing which he himself appears to have experienced.
He calls it specialism (from *speculum*, the mirror or
means of estimating a thing by seeing it in its entirety,
hence, seeing all at one glance). Walt Whitman, who
may be said to have had as powerful a redirecting influence upon American thought and letters as any poet who
has lived among us, speaks of the flash of light, the
illumination which transformed all his seeing.

These are a few of the type of individual to whom

Bucke goes for enlightenment upon his problem. There are many others included in the volume, among them Dante, Las Casas, Yepes, Francis Bacon, Behmen, William Blake, Edward Carpenter, Pascal, Spinoza, Emerson, Thoreau, Richard Jeffries.

Probably there is no one today but would grant that these men, for the most part, stand head and shoulders above the average of mankind. Disagreement might arise as to the source of their power. Thus, for example, the rationalist might deny to Jesus his divine sonship, or to Plotinus his mystical ecstasies, but he would hardly deny to these men their real moral greatness.

The Secret of Their Greatness

Wherein lay the secret of their superiority? That is the problem to which Bucke addresses himself. His answer, whether true or false—and we must remember that his book was a pioneering venture—is sufficiently arresting to call for our serious consideration. Studying the life histories of these men, he finds in all of them— sometimes in greater degree, sometimes in less—a clearly marked phenomenon of consciousness. These men do not reason their way to conclusions, although reason— the search for truth—apparently played a part in preparation for their final insight. In every case they experienced what, for want of a better term, we may call "illumination."

Gautama, so the accounts indicate—and in the following cases the historic accounts are not, of course, all equally reliable—experienced it under the Bo tree; Paul on the road to Damascus; Jesus as the heavens were rent asunder and the Spirit descended upon him out of the heavens saying, "Thou art my Beloved Son; in thee I am well pleased"; Plotinus in the three transforming "ecstasies" which he experienced during his lifetime; Mohammed in his cavern of meditation on Mount Hara; John Yepes in his monk's cell; Las Casas as he read the mass and a light seemed to shine upon him, utterly changing his life; Jacob Behmen, the cobbler, as he sat looking upon a burnished pewter dish and fell into an inward ecstasy, the effects of which remained with him throughout his subsequent life, transforming him from an ordinary workman into a man of such insight that he remains to this day one of the outstanding spiritual geniuses of the race. Though not all of the historical testimony is of equal value—some of it is hardly to be accepted—there is enough that is authenticated to give grounds for the conclusion that these men experienced in similar fashion.

We may, to be sure, brush these experiences aside as aberrations. William James, however, warns us that it will not do to pooh-pooh them entirely away. Average minds may do that, and, in fact, do do it, but not scientific minds, to whom the extraordinary is simply an invitation to investigate and try to understand. But there is a particular reason why we are stopped from brushing these experiences aside. These men do not act after the manner of men suffering from an aberration. Out of them has come a great portion of the spiritual wisdom of the race. They are, as it were, among the illuminati of mankind. If "by their fruits ye shall know them," these men have shown fruits so far above the average as to make them spiritual leaders of mankind.

That which occurred to them, and the resultant views of life and the universe which they achieved, must be accepted, then, as authentic enough at least to merit investigation. Keeping in mind also that the average individual is still, in the main, on a lesser plane of development, we shall not be at all surprised if occurrences which take place in those who have apparently, even in a small degree, emerged to a higher level of insight, are regarded as signs either of supernatural power or of psychic disorder. Is it not possible, on the other hand, to regard these occurrences as signs simply of a higher stage of the very same typical development through which all of us are passing?

How This New Consciousness Functions

Realizing, then, that we are dealing with superior minds, we may ask what manner of conscious life it was that they seemed to achieve, and what it was that they reported. A number of facts, according to Bucke, are to be noted. In all the outstanding cases, there is a time— coming invariably in the maturity of life and after a long preparatory stage of exploration—of swift illumination. Most often there is a sense of actual light, sometimes so bright that the individual seems to be stricken temporarily blind. In other cases, the illumina-

tion is more of an inward nature, the darkness of ignorance and misconception seeming to fall away before
the illuminating glow. Following the experience of the
light there is a sudden intellectual clarification. Things
are understood that were not understood before. This is
strikingly in evidence in the case of the cobbler, Jacob
Behmen, and of Gautama. The whole scheme of things
takes on meaning and significance. There is, as it were,
a grasp of the clue to life and the universe. With
this, in every case, goes a moral exaltation. This itself
is significant. If it is true that the emergence into
self-consciousness (our average level) out of pre-self-
consciousness meant the emergence into moral consciousness, this further development marks the emergence
to a still higher level of moral life. This is incontestable in the case of such men as Jesus, Gautama, Mohammed, Socrates, Plotinus, Las Casas, John Yepes,
Dante, Whitman. In many cases the moral exaltation is
so great as to arouse the traditional moralities to opposi-
tion. Jesus was crucified, Mohammed was persecuted,
Socrates was condemned to death, Whitman has been
reviled as "immoral." This is wholly to be expected, since
moral values on the plane above the self-conscious can
as yet hardly be understood by those who are still on
that level where each individual is primarily himself
and *not* any other. For the moral exaltation is particularly
characterized by a sense of oneness with the all. The
sharp division lines of individuality which we find in our
average life drop away, and the individual, without indeed losing his individuality, becomes vitally a part of

all life and lives in that apparently impossible oneness
of existence. This is what Gautama meant by (the usually
misunderstood) state of Nirvana.

But it is also noteworthy in the case of every one
of these men that, in their moral exaltation, the fear of
death vanishes completely. There is, instead, a sense of
the utter livingness of reality. Bucke thus describes the
typical experience:

"He does not come to believe merely; but he sees
and knows that the cosmos, which to the self-conscious
mind seems made up of dead matter, is in fact far otherwise—is in very truth a living presence. He sees that
instead of men being, as it were, patches of life scattered
through an infinite sea of non-living substance, they are
in reality specks of relative death in an infinite ocean of
life. He sees that the life of man is eternal, as all life is
eternal . . . that the foundation principle of the world
is what we call love, and that the happiness of every individual is in the long run absolutely certain. . . . Especially does he obtain such a conception of the WHOLE,
or at least of an immense WHOLE as dwarfs all
conception, imagination, or speculation, springing from
or belonging to ordinary self-consciousness, such a conception as makes the old attempts mentally to grasp
the universe and its meaning petty and even ridiculous." [2]

No wonder Plotinus called it *ecstasis*, ecstasy. No
wonder the mind that calls a spade a spade calls it moon-
madness. However, we are not here seeking to prove
anything. We are simply indicating the apparent facts

[2] *Ibid.,* p. 73.

of the case from the study of these individuals. This is the kind of experience that each of these men apparently achieves and the kind of meaning that reality assumes for them. Whether we go back several thousand years to Gautama, or come forward, in our own day, to Whitman, the meaning that existence has for these men is always fundamentally the same.

Out of the Cave?

Let us return to the striking passage quoted above: "He (this suddenly illumined mind) sees that instead of men being, as it were, patches of life scattered through an infinite sea of non-living substance, they are in reality specks of relative death in an infinite ocean of life." Here, indeed, is a curious inversion of ideas. We normally believe that the process of life is an inevitable process toward death. We—so we think—are the living ones. We living ones go toward that which will eventually swallow us up in the utter stillness of the non-living. These men completely reverse that picture. We, so they tell us, are the comparatively dead. We have deadness within us—untruth, ugliness, evil. The process of our life is the process of escaping relative death and going toward the really living.

Whether true or false, it is at least an arresting thought. We are reminded again of Plato's analogy of the Cave. Here in this cave-like life of ours, said Plato, we have commerce with shadows. We think the shadows to be real and to be living. We think, therefore, that we

ourselves are authentically, indubitably alive. That belief, Plato suggests, is erroneous. Let one of us escape
from the cave and he will behold a world so alive in its
reality that he will be transported by the beauty and the
wonder of it, and he will hurry back to his cave-fellows
to tell them how comparatively dead their existence is.

The Logic of It All

Regarded from the point of view of sober logic what
is here suggested seems not improbable. Man has already
evolved to a plane of life above the inorganic, the plant,
and the animal. He has achieved self-consciousness. It
is wholly conceivable that he is to advance beyond the
limited and inevitably distorting status of mere self-
consciousness. Such an advance, of course, will not mean
the supersession of the previous stages. For even at the
self-conscious stage man still retains his earlier powers
of perception and simple sensitivity. These, so to speak,
have been "lifted up" to the higher level of self-
consciousness. So, likewise, we may suppose that eventually, in far greater fulness than is now true among us,
man's self-consciousness will be lifted up to the higher
level of what Bucke chooses to call "cosmic consciousness."

What, now, is most characteristic of the self-conscious
plane, and what (if we can trust the reports) will be
characteristic of a plane of consciousness that at once
includes and transcends self-consciousness?

The outstanding nature of self-consciousness is implied in the term. It is *self*-consciousness. It is the kind of consciousness that sharply distinguishes the self from its world. It is therefore a highly individuating form of life. It makes me aware of the "me" and you of the "you." (Note that I have mentioned myself first.) It makes me aware of the fact that first and foremost I am not you. I am myself. And it makes you aware that you are not I. You are yourself.

Self-consciousness, in short, makes us arrange ourselves as a kind of world of psychic atoms—each himself and not the other. We move toward one another or away from one another, bump into one another, shove one another out of the way, love one another or hate one another. Whatever we do, the outstanding quality of us is that each is first of all himself. Only quite secondarily does each yield a little of himself—his attention and interest—to others.

It would seem possible to believe that if man is to evolve to a yet higher level, it will be toward a form of conscious life in which this overemphasis of the self is corrected. And this is precisely what seems to take place in the lives of the men we have mentioned. Both their intellectual illumination and their moral exaltation are in a direction away from separateness of selfhood. In each case they gain a sense of the whole, of the intrinsic, interpenetrating *oneness* of a living reality. In every case this sense of wholeness breaks down the barriers of their separate selfhood, and they feel themselves in indisseverable union with all their fellows and with all the universe.

Thus we might say that man is moving toward that kind of consciousness in which there is a greater integration of the self with its world. All this is apparently verified by what we have come to believe to be the truer forms of human existence. Thus we take it for granted that the unified individual is a more capable individual than the disunified one, that the individual who can surrender himself to a great love is on a higher plane than he who never breaks through the shell of his separate individuality, that the individual whose interest goes out in relationship to his community is greater than he who remains isolated within his own concerns, that the individual who can be world-minded is greater than he who can be only local-minded.

Thus even on our average plane we recognize that the true direction of life is toward living into a larger wholeness of life. We sometimes express it as the progress from the ego-centric (the child's normal condition), to the increasingly socio-centric life—love, home, community, nation, world. The level of conscious life which Bucke describes is then simply a further stage in this progression. It is the stage in which the individual becomes vividly one with the universe. And because he becomes one with the universe he is transformed in all his being so that he becomes vividly one with his fellows.

Apparently this is the type of human life that, in our best moments, we have dimly previsioned—the life not torn apart into self-assertive, self-demanding, loudly vociferating entities, but the life joined together in the blessedness of a living unity. Jesus taught that life. So did Gautama. So did Plotinus. So did all these men who achieved this apparently higher level of experience. At least in this respect they were not deluded.

It would be a grave error, however, to think of the experiences thus described as separating these men from our common humanity, and of relegating the rest of us to a hopelessly lower level. Rather, those experiences seem to illuminate what is significant in the life of man. In the foregoing chapters we have seen man as the endless quester after that which, however momentarily achieved, is nevertheless ever beyond him. What is all his endless quest but a wish to unite himself with a reality which is immeasurably greater than himself? The foundation principle of the world, then, would indeed seem to be love, if we mean by love the urge to identify oneself with that which is beyond oneself and alluringly greater than oneself. Whether it be in the quest of the True, or the Beautiful, or the Good, in the creative passion of personal love, or in those high heroisms in which man yields himself in an utter devotion, the authentic movement is toward a oneness with what is loved. And whenever that movement is strong in him, there is no sense of deadness; there is a sense, rather, of kinship with what is far more living. Thus the most significant movement of man's experience would seem to be away from relative death to that which is more enduringly and veritably alive.

Chapter XIX

THE FATE OF VALUES

"I CRIED over beautiful things knowing no beautiful thing lasts." [1] That has been the plaint of the poet—indeed, the plaint of us all. What utter tragedy of waste! we cry. Beauty that vanishes, nobility moldered in the dust, passionate love that lies as dead bones in a coffin! Where do they all go? What becomes of them? Is life the transiently futile thing that it seems to be? Is all that we deeply care for doomed to a fatal extinction—"shoveled into the tombs," as the same poet expresses it—dropped like soundless plummets into the void?

Perhaps our difficulty lies in a peculiar inability to follow the destiny of values beyond their time-and-space embodiment. We see beauty made incarnate in marble or in color; we hear it in its embodiment of poetry or music; we listen to wisdom clothed in words. When these vanish, they seem to vanish utterly. And yet another poet stoutly maintains:

---

[1] Carl Sandburg, "Autumn Movement," in *Cornhuskers*, p. 16 (Holt).

"A thing of beauty is a joy forever:
Its loveliness increases; it will never
Pass into nothingness." [2]

Is there in some sense an indestructibility of values, or are values paradoxical realities that pass into nullity, leaving no trace behind?

How Values Live On

If we say yes to the second part of the foregoing sentence, we are faced with the incomprehensibility of a reality that can become an utter unreality. If we answer yes to the first part, we are faced with the puzzle of giving form and substance to something that in fact has vanished. How shall we resolve this peculiar difficulty?

Let us consider, as an example, the illuminating insight achieved by Gautama under the Bo tree. Gautama held it "in his mind," as we say, for a number of years, giving it expression in his teaching. Then he died. Did the insight die? Obviously, in one sense, we know that it did not die. It lived on in its effects. And it still lives on. In countless ways the world is now different because of the one-time reality of this insight. As a psychological phenomenon in a particular individual, indeed, the insight seems to have vanished; but as incorporated into the processes of the world, it will apparently go on perpetuating itself.

In like manner, we might say that Socrates' thoughts

[2] Keats, *Endymion*, Book I.

continue to endure. They have been woven into the processes of life. Here in the twentieth century is a young man who has suddenly taken on a new lease of life after reading the account of Socrates' challenge to his jurors. The value, then, that Socrates generated over two thousand years ago still endures and is actually operating in the living world.

In like manner may one not say that everything that has been experienced as beautiful continues on in its effects? To have aroused a response is to have set something going in the world. The thing of beauty, therefore, is more than that which is contained within its own particular space-time limits. It becomes an operative force in an environment; its origin passes away, but it, itself, does not.

This is doubtless what Goethe meant when he wrote:

"Kein Wesen kann zu nichts zerfallen,
     Das Ewige regt sich fort in allen."

When he spoke of *Wesen*—essences—he was no doubt thinking of those values that find their place in our life and that prove their authenticity by being able to belong to it lastingly.

Values as Augmentative

But we are now brought to a further consideration. The true thoughts of all the great individuals among us, from the beginning of known history, have not only endured in their effects, but, so far as we can conceive, they have progressively added to the value-content of our world. It seems an incomprehensible statement to make that the value-content of the world is exactly the same since Jesus and Plato spoke as it was in the Neanderthal days or the days before man was on this earth. It may indeed be true, as scientists have maintained, that, so far as physical matter is concerned, nothing is ever added. It seems meaningless to say the same about values. When new values come, they add to the value-content and the value-configuration of the world.

How will this affect our conception of the universe? If it is true that every new achievement of beauty is so much added to the value-content of the world, that every great love, every new integrity, every new aspiration is so much added, then reality must be conceived as something that grows progressively richer in content.

There are, of course, metaphysical perplexities in this thought. The objection might be made that it relies upon creation out of nothing. If these new values, it will be said, were not there before, then, apparently, they have actually come to be out of what was not previously there. In other words, they have been created out of nothing.

The answer to this would seem to be that while these actual, realized values were not there before, their possibility was. Possibility, as we have before indicated, is a type of reality. The possibility of a child was in the bodies of its two parents before it was born. But the child itself was not in those bodies. Thus when the child comes, a possibility is transformed into an actuality. A new reality enters the world—not, however, *ex nihilo*, but *ex potentia*. May we not say the same of these new values? The possibility of them was, indeed, always there, but they had never yet been brought to actuality. Now, by some happy circumstance—the birth, let us say, of a rare individual—the possibilities are transformed into actualities, and new values enter the world.

In this sense the universe is at the same time always what it has been and always becomes what it never was before. The paradox would seem to be resolved when we admit the reality of possibility. As a world of measureless possibility, the universe is eternally the same; but as a process in which possibility is being transformed into new actuality, the universe is forever augmenting.

Conclusion

We may return, then, to our opening paragraph. "I cried over beautiful things knowing no beautiful thing lasts." But in a very real sense it does last. And in the very nature of things it must add new richness to the world.

It is at least not impossible nor illogical to think in this way. We noted, in the preceding chapter, how one after another of those who achieved the experience we there described, sensed the fact that the reality that encompasses us is far more living than our present lives, that it is indeed the more vital life out of which all vitality comes. But we also note that all that is greatly vital in our lives goes into this encompassing life, aug-

menting it in the degree that it has the qualities which
fundamentally endure.

"Candle flame buffeted by darkness,
  The slow curve of purple iris petal,
  Rainbow arch above the water-fall . . .
  These I have seen—and these have passed away . . .
  Have passed . . . whither?
  Into the Great Nothing?

"Then fearless shall I face the baffling void . . .
  For how shall Nothing take unto itself
  All lovely things,
  All fragile things that fade,
  And not itself become
  Majestic,
  Clothed in wonder?" [3]

[3] Bonaro Wilkinson, *Unlost.*

Chapter XX

GOD AND THE MODERN MAN

CONSIDERING THE PROBLEM AFRESH

"THAT Man is the product of causes which had no prevision of the end they were achieving; that his origin, his growth, his hopes and fears, his loves and his beliefs, are but the outcome of accidental collocations of atoms; that no fire, no heroism, no intensity of thought and feeling, can preserve an individual life beyond the grave; that all the labors of the ages, all the devotion, all the inspiration, all the noonday brightness of human genius, are destined to extinction in the vast death of the solar system, and that the whole temple of Man's achievement must inevitably be buried beneath the débris of a universe in ruins— all these things, if not quite beyond dispute, are yet so nearly certain, that no philosophy which rejects them can hope to stand. Only within the scaffolding of these truths, only on the firm foundation of unyielding despair, can the soul's habitation henceforth be safely built." [1]

These words were written in 1902. They are perhaps the most poignant expression of that utter re-

[1] Bertrand Russell, "A Free Man's Worship, in *Mysticism and Logic,* p. 47 (W. W. Norton & Company, Inc.).

nunciation of all man's enduring hopes which was the
logical outcome of the science of the nineteenth century. Looked at from the vantage point of three decades
of new science, one wonders how the incredible view
could ever have been held. A universe in ultimate
ruin!—and within this universe now on the way to ruin
a creature, born out of its inherent life, strong enough
and fearless enough to fling it a defiance.

We remember the reasons for this view. Physical
science had formulated the second law of thermodynamics, the law of entropy, or the degradation of energy. All energy, according to this law, tends to run
down. In the end, the energy of the world will have
descended to its lowest level, and the universe will be
locked in the icy stillness of an eternal death.

What hope, then, for man? "Brief and powerless is
Man's life; on him and all his race the slow, sure doom
falls pitiless and dark. Blind to good and evil, reckless
of destruction, omnipotent matter rolls on its relentless
way; for Man, condemned today to lose his dearest,
tomorrow himself to pass through the gate of darkness, it remains only to cherish, ere yet the blow falls,
the lofty thoughts that ennoble his days; disdaining the
coward terrors of the slave of Fate, to worship at the
shrine that his own hands have built; undismayed by
the empire of chance, to preserve a mind free from the
wanton tyranny that rules his outward life; proudly
defiant of the irresistible forces that tolerate, for a moment, his knowledge and his condemnation, to sustain
alone, a weary but unyielding Atlas, the world that his

own ideals have fashioned despite the trampling march of unconscious power." [2]

There is perhaps in all modern literature no nobler expression than this of the courage of despair. It gives the lie to those who proclaim that materialism, and with it, atheism, spell the end of all greatness in man. And yet, noble as it is, one wonders if it is true. We recall the remarkable series of discoveries made by the physical scientists in the later years of the nineteenth century and the early years of the twentieth, discoveries which overturned the sure finality of the physical views that had reigned throughout most of the century. We recall the birth of a new physics, exploring energies undreamed of by the older mechanical science. We recall the development of a view that novel configurations of life and mind are generated within the cosmic process. From the standpoint of emergent evolution there is no appearance of the universe running down, but rather of its creating out of itself new and more vital forms. Finally, we recall the warnings issued to us by the scientists themselves that we must not, from a knowledge of a part of the universe, judge the whole. Physics may indeed have found its law of entropy. But physics deals with an exceedingly small range of reality. To pattern all the rest of the world upon what is found on the physical level is to commit the grave fallacy of abstraction.

Thus it seems possible now to challenge the courageous gloom of the view just quoted. Russell himself, in

[2] *Ibid.*, p. 56.

his own thinking, has advanced with the later science, but his essay still remains printed and widely read.[3] It may have to go the way of that part of the nineteenth-century science which is outmoded. For in the twentieth century, we are at last permitted to regard psychological life as of a significance as fundamental as that of inorganic matter.

The Upward Trend of Life and Mind

When, now, without materialistic bias, we examine organic and psychological life, we seem to discover that instead of entropy (a turning in) being their outstanding characteristic, that which we might call, by contrast, ektropy (a turning out) is predominant. The entire process of organic evolution seems to justify such a conclusion. Organic life is a development, not only in the individual, but in the species. It grows more complicated in its structure, more diverse in its contacts, more capable in its adjustments. It goes, so to speak, not downward but upward. And when we turn to psychological life, we note the same process in even more marked degree. A single, apparently insignificant individual, James Watt, observes the steam issuing from the tea kettle, and a simple thought of his causes

[3] He writes, in the Preface of the 1929 edition: "The two essays on 'A Free Man's Worship' and 'The Study of Mathematics' depend upon a metaphysic which is more platonic than that which I now believe in. . . . Pragmatically, however, I still see a certain value in the mood expressed in 'A Free Man's Worship,' since it is calculated to be useful in times of stress and to reinforce a desirable kind of obstinacy in the face of obstacles."

a new civilization to come into being. Another apparently insignificant individual, Rousseau, in a slim volume launches an idea, and through it contributes to the overthrow of an age-old oppression and the building up of a new order of life. In such cases the results seem utterly incommensurable with the physical stimuli. In brief, a new kind of initiating agency has appeared which, while accommodating itself to the physical laws, is not completely subject to them. Psychological life, when it enters upon the scene, is powerfully like that Demon which Clerk Maxwell ingeniously imagined as the operative agent that might turn the downward processes of the unguided physical world into upward processes, thereby neutralizing the effects of the law of the degradation of energy.

In the foregoing chapters we have noted some of the ways in which the ektropic or upbuilding process functions. In generating truth, beauty, and goodness, we discovered the power in ourselves, through the achievement of various coherences, to establish in the world new realities that are of enduring value. In love, we noted a process of begetting whereby out of two comes more than the two. In man at his best, we found the will to pass beyond his present inadequate self, the will to yield his present self for the realization of what is greater than himself.

And so we can turn once more to a fresh facing of the fundamental issue of all life and death. What really is the nature of the universe? Need we any longer believe, as hitherto we seemed compelled to do, that the nature of the universe is such that "the things we care for most are at the mercy of the things we care for least"? [4] In short, we come to the question of a God.

Clearing Away Misconceptions

There will be the need, first, for a clearing away of old religious misconceptions. Much that man once believed about God (or gods) we can obviously no longer believe. If we regard the older ideas (many of them still entertained by individuals and sects), we realize that they were fashioned upon the patterns of the kind of life that man was then living. In the centuries when he was little more than an animal, ringed by terrors and incredibly ignorant and weak, the gods were monstrous creatures to be feared. When his life became more settled and organized into communities, his gods were transformed into rulers. As the organization of his life was increasingly consolidated, the several rulers became one Ruler. In the patriarchal stage of consolidation, the god was a Patriarch, a Father. In the monarchical stages, he was a King. In the first stage of sheer terror, the gods were of such a nature that the chief energies of man's life were spent in placating them. In the period of organized society, his chief energies were spent in obeying them (or him).

None of these beliefs about the deity will any longer adequately serve us. Even the belief with which we have grown familiar, of God as a Heavenly Father,

[4] Montague, W. P., *Belief Unbound*, p. 66 (Yale University Press).

who orders our welfare and expects from us adoration and obedience, is, from the modern point of view, inadequate.

Two Further Shortcomings

We note two further shortcomings in these views. The first is the externality of the relationship supposed to exist between man and deity. Deity—Jupiter, Thor, Jehovah—is a creature who is not man. Man, in his turn, is a creature who dwells outside the compass of divine life. The Deity rules him, sets laws for him, shapes his fate for him, demands obedience and adoration of him. Man is here, God is there.

All this goes counter to our modern conviction of the intrinsic oneness of the world. We are no longer willing to think in terms of the dualism of the supernatural and the natural. We are convinced naturalists. We believe that we are in and of the world and that the world is in and of us. Whatever God is—if indeed He is—He must be conceived as moving in our members. He must be thought of as of the very essential life of ourselves and we as of the very essential life of Him. The old externalistic expressions, then, will no longer serve. To call God King, Ruler, even Father, puts us in danger of missing the sheer interpenetrativeness of the world in which we live.

The second inadequacy resulted from the peculiar backwardness of man's former life. He was densely ignorant of the world. The best he could do was to make some precarious adjustment to its requirements. He hunted for the food that roamed the fields, or he ate of the food yielded him by the soil. The world was all there. So far as he was concerned, it was a finished thing. To his ignorance, there was no thought that the world itself is a continuously growing, transforming reality. It was easy, therefore, for him to conceive of an initial Creator. Moreover, to his incapacity, there was no thought that he held powers within himself that could change the world into new forms. It was natural, therefore, for him to conceive of himself simply as a recipient of divine favors. God was the giver of all good things, and man's proper relation to Him was to yield Him gratitude and praise.

It is these inadequacies, in the main, against which the "atheist" has contended, and rightly. But when we have cast out these inadequate conceptions of deity, is there nothing that remains save pure negation?

Re-thinking the Problem

Apparently we must re-think the problem in modern terms. From our present point of view of a world evolving, is there any ground for believing in a God? Let us employ an expression used by Professor Montague. By God, we shall mean a "power greater than ourselves which makes for good." Is there any ground for believing in the reality of such a power?

Nineteenth-century science, as we saw, confining itself to purely physical investigation, believed in a process that made for eventual ruin. Twentieth-century thinking, as we have likewise seen, thinks of a world not going to ruin, but developing into new forms. If this later thought is true, there is, then, an upthrust in nature, a power of self-augmentation. As we note this self-augmentation developing into organic life and eventually into that powerful initiating source of new configurations which we call psychological life, we are led to the question: Is not this the true nature of reality? Is there not in nature an *élan*, a quickening vitality, an urge toward more widely functioning wholes? And is not this what we can mean by the reality of God?

If we answer in the affirmative, we shall not, however, make the mistake of setting this quickening vitality apart from ourselves as a Creature that rules us. This vitality, we have seen, is in ourselves, as it is in all nature. There are times when we do not respond to it. We refuse to let it work in us. We remain static. We even hinder the realization of what is better; we actually initiate the worse. Not only, therefore, is this quickening vitality not something apart from us, but, also, it is not omnipotent, for it is constantly being obstructed. But the whole process of our life seems to show that it is the eventually triumphant power. The "worse," as we have seen, is its own worst enemy. It has disintegration in its members. It goes down to defeat and to increasing defeat. The *élan* of life, apparently, is toward truth, beauty, and goodness, for these have within them the lasting power that lies in coherence.

Planes of Reality

Have we now, in this quickening vitality, found what we can mean by God? And can we further describe this God? Let us recall our former caution. On the human plane, we said, we see as humans and think as humans. There appears to be no way in which we can transport ourselves to the point of view of a plane of existence far beyond our own. Must we not say, then, that any effort adequately to describe this quickening vitality of the universe must meet with defeat?

Let us return, however, to our former suggestion. It was to the effect that what we find to be of significance on our human plane must be in correlation with significances beyond the human. What we have a right to do, then, is to find on our human level that which is of supreme worth and let that stand as a dim adumbration of the Highest.

When is man at his best? Obviously he is so as he makes his effort to achieve an increasingly wider and intenser wholeness of life. He is at his best in the enduringness of this effort: he is the "mortal nature seeking as far as is possible to be everlasting and immortal." He is at his best in the creativeness of this effort: he is seeking to reorganize life in more fruitful ways.

Our Sense of God

Here, then, we seem to have the most authentic clue to the nature of that quickening vitality of the universe

which we would call God. God is, in infinite degree,
the everlasting creative life that moves toward wholeness.

Obviously, everything that is of significance has come
out of this quickening vitality of the universe. In the
upthrust of centuries, life, mind, and personality have
come. It would be strange, then, to accord to this cosmic *élan* less than that which has emerged from its own
being. However, we shall err if we say that God is mind
and personality. That, again, would be patterning
upon the human. But may we not say that mind and
personality are in this quickening vitality just as truly
as we can say that this quickening vitality is in mind
and personality? This that we see as the ektropic power
of the universe is indeed personality, but is as far more
than personality as the cosmic is beyond the merely
human. Since, however, personality is the highest form
of reality which we can contemplate, may we not be
permitted, in our inadequate and metaphorical human
way, to speak of this cosmic *élan* in personal terms?

There is, however, an immediate danger in this, for
we shall at once be tempted to set this Person over
against ourselves. We must keep to the difficult task
of conceiving of this vitality not as an individual over
against ourselves, but as a life in which we live and
which itself lives in us.

If the divine is the quickening life in us, then we
devote ourselves to that life in the degree that we respond to the deep impulse within us toward creative
integration. This is far different from the traditional

meaning of devoting ourselves by prayer and ceremony to a Deity who is afar in the heavens. On the contrary, this God is a life within ourselves. Again, we love this God in the degree that we love the life that is creatively uniting. This is very different from loving a Father in the heavens and at the same time, on earth, exploiting or killing our fellows. To love God is to love the processes of bringing life into a more vital integration. The scientist, in this sense, loves God as he ranges out into the universe to unite his mind with the yet unknown realities. In similar sense, the teacher loves God, as, standing before his class, he seeks to unite his hearers and himself in a oneness of understanding. The mother loves God as she loves to integrate her life with the life of her child. Wherever, in short, there is the process of vital integration, there is God. Wherever there is a passionate love of integrating, there is the passionate love of God.

The Transforming Experience

There is a greatness about the realization of this that is like nothing else. If what we have described is true, we are in the infinite and the infinite is in us. All our enduring quest then gets its explanation and its significance. It is the God operative within ourselves. As, then, we discover the more enduring values, or as we create them, we enact God in our own lives.

We can, as we know, close our lives to this quickening vitality, or we can open them. We close them when we refuse to respond to the call of new possibilities. We open them when we seek to bring to birth out of infinite potentiality actualities that are greater than those we have hitherto achieved.

"If that is in truth what an authentic religious experience would mean, or could mean," writes Professor Montague, "then for those who object to religion there remains but one possible line—they must deny that there is such a thing. Of course, it would be good, they will say, if it were real, but it is not real; it is but a revival of ancient empty hopes masking its emptiness in phrases. Abandon it and let us give what time and energy we have to our real business of living like mortals in a world which none but mortals inhabit. To this we can only reply: Perhaps you are right, but there is a chance that you are not. There is at least a chance that there is an upward-trending power in nature to account for such adaptations as we find. There is at least a chance that the cosmos as a whole has a unitary life and consciousness, and that the evolutionary *nisus* is its will which, though not omnipotent, is omnipresent. And lastly, if there is a kind of stillness, and if one can contrive a queer little turn of the heart away from what one knows to be mean, there is a chance, however small, that a union with the holy spirit of this Promethean God will be attained, and that, by such a union, one's world would be made radiant, and one's life become a high romance." [5]

[5] *Ibid.* p. 97.

Chapter XXI

A COMING SYNTHESIS

THE NEW TREND OF THOUGHT

"WE seem to be arriving at a time," writes Edward Carpenter, "when, with the circling of our knowledge of the globe, a great synthesis of all human thought . . . is quite naturally and inevitably taking place. . . . Out of this meeting of elements is already arising the dim outline of a philosophy which must surely dominate human thought for a long period." [1]

It is interesting to trace the course which our modern intellectual life has followed. The scientific thought of the nineteenth century was like a wave. First came physics. Then, in the middle of the century, biology was swept into the strong current of materialistic thinking. Finally, in the latter part of the century, psychology, casting "psyche" overboard (*Psychologie ohne Seele*), cut loose from its ancient moorings and allowed itself to be swept into the powerful current.

This takes us well toward and into the twentieth century. And now it was the novelists and litterateurs who were swept into the materialistic wave. They seemed to be influenced first by the new psychologists,

---

[1] Edward Carpenter, *The Art of Creation*, p. vii (Macmillan).

with the consequence that the romantic scales fell from their eyes. Influenced by the biologists, they saw man as in reality little more than a primitive animal. Influenced by the physicists, they beheld the entire universe as mindless and purposeless. So they were carried along. As a result, they grew adept at keeping their eyes upon the down-going or entropic trends of life. They learned to note banality, drabness, meanness. They beheld the human scene as one unillumined and uninspired by anything that is up-going or ektropic. Even love, the greatest, apparently, of man's transforming powers, they reduced to a paltry animal passion. And that out-reaching quality of mind and will whereby man conquers for himself new worlds, they analyzed with merciless realism into a lust for power.

Through the writings of such novelists and litterateurs, the philosophy of a universe emptied of value achieved a vogue it never could have gained from scientists or philosophers. It set for all manner of minds the approved attitude. It disposed of man's enthusiasms. It made ideals unfashionable and cynicism the mark of the sophisticate. And so it was that scientific materialism came to its culminating expression in the romances of the unromantic and the illusions of the disillusioned.

The Second Wave

But meanwhile, as we remember, something significant was happening. While this wave of scientific

materialism was at its height, and while the courage of
realistic despair was riding the crest, physics was making new discoveries. Suddenly the crest of the wave
broke, and physics was swept down into the trough of
new doubts but also of new possibilities. One might
say that the first three decades of the twentieth century were the period of the down-wash and the trough.
Much of the older materialism poured on into those
decades, although, because of the new discoveries, the
justification for materialism was gone.

And now we may bring the story to date. The upward movement of a new wave is beginning. Physics,
once in the forward sweep of materialistic thinking, is
now in the forward sweep of anti-materialistic thinking. Biology has not as yet in full measure felt the
power of this new up-going wave. But it begins to feel
it. Especially in the recognition of a creative emergence,
biology enters upon a non-materialistic view of the life-
processes. Psychology, which, as we noted, was the
latest of the sciences to be swept into the current of
that earlier thinking, is still reluctant to make itself
into a science of what is uniquely psychological. Doubtless its earlier mishaps with the "soul" are still too recent in its memory. But even in psychology there is a
trend away from purely mechanistic conceptions to such
as admit the organismic character of psychological life.

Thus a new wave is sweeping into our twentieth century. The novelists and litterateurs of whom we have
spoken are now the real mid-Victorians. For they remain the literary spokesmen of a nineteenth-century

materialism which is so thoroughly of the past that scientists scarcely grant it a passing thought. Is it extravagant to believe that as the new wave gains momentum and power, it will carry away the entropic despairs that have characterized the past few decades, bringing to human life a conception of its more authentic potentialities?

The Contributions of Materialism

There is at least the possibility, then, that in not many more decades a new synthesis may be achieved on the basis of the essentially living and continuously creative character of the universe. Toward the accomplishment of this the recent interlude of materialistic science will have been of very great moment. It will have made impossible a return to naïve anthropomorphic conceptions. Anyone who has seriously passed through nineteenth-century scientific thinking will have gained an impersonality of outlook and a skepticism about unverified assumptions which will emancipate him from the kind of subjectivistic illusions that have been so powerful to hinder and distort man's thinking.

It will have done more. There is a body of profoundly significant thought which comes out of the East. But the expression of that thought is more frequently than not distasteful to the western thinker. It is, in the main, directly assertive of ultimate truths.

It states conclusions without patiently building up the evidence for them.

It is non-experimental. It has the tone of "thus saith the Seer." It seeks to impress by its note of deep mystery and of a penetration into realms beyond the compass of average human experience. Eastern philosophy, one suspects, has had small effect upon western thought chiefly because of its manner. But there is every reason to believe that as the influence of western thinking—particularly its experimental hard-headedness—is felt in the East, a new philosophic manner will be adopted, and the profound spirituality of eastern thought will be expressed in ways more acceptable to the western mind.

There is also a body of thought in the western world which is of real significance but which has latterly been neglected—that of the mystics. The techniques of nineteenth-century materialism will have their effect likewise upon this thought. They will be a challenge to its vaporous unclarity, its uncritical mixing together of subjectivistic fantasy and veritable experience. As a result, mysticism, more critically equipped, may yet enter our modern thought and impart to it a greater reach and depth.

Changes in the Social Order

Meanwhile significant changes are taking place in our industrial, political, social, educational, and religious life. We have definitely passed out of the crude stage of nineteenth-century industrialism. The older industrialism made materialism its ally and excuse. The industrialism of today is increasingly being furthered in the spirit of preserving and enhancing human values.

In like manner, we have definitely passed out of the crudest stage of nineteenth-century nationalism. That older nationalism made the theory of a struggle for survival its ally and excuse. To grow strong and defeat other nations seemed the very wisdom of nature itself. But a new political insight is developing in which the conception of nations joined together in the common enterprise of advancing the life of man is becoming axiomatic among us.

Similarly, education is undergoing important transformations. From a relatively external process of pouring in facts, it is increasingly becoming a process of evoking the deeper, generative possibilities that lie within the individual.

Changes are occurring, also, within the social sphere. The animadversions of novelists and social critics disclosing the relative banality of life are accepted as a kind of challenge, arousing us to a profounder research into what life may be.

Finally, religion is moving out of its old temples of anthropomorphic supernaturalism and learning to face facts. The old fight between science and religion (save among some backward souls) is really at an end. The alert religionist is no longer afraid of new truth. He seeks it.

The Arts

Meanwhile the last few decades have witnessed important changes in the realm of the fine arts. In many cases these have produced bewildering results, so that frequently we look upon pictures of the modern type or listen to modern music or poetry and wonder what has come over the world that such apparently meaningless creations should be accepted as serious works of art.

When, however, we realize what is happening, even these bewildering results gain a certain significance. They have the same kind of significance that attaches to the unfamiliar mechanisms one finds in an inventor's workshop. Often these turn out to be ludicrous failures. Sometimes, however, grotesque as they at first seem to unaccustomed eyes, they are found to embody surprising new masteries of latent forces.

The world of art today is most easily understood when it is regarded as an inventor's workshop. The age of fixed standards and stereotyped forms is, temporarily at least, at an end. Artists sense new possibilities. Their art, whether in painting, sculpture, music, or poetry, is not simply a childish striving for novelty. It is the outcome of the conviction that the art forms hitherto achieved are inadequate. Thus, when the musical inventor experiments with his dissonances, he is not attempting simply to shock unaccustomed ears. He is trying to express life more fully than in the pretty, closed harmonies of many of the older forms. Life as we now behold it and live it has all the confusion of a new emergent, but it is confusion seeking its way to a new kind of organization and integration.

This, one suspects, is the clue to the modern movement in the arts. It is a movement away from closed forms. Closed forms are static, finished, and therefore clear. The modern movement breaks through closed into open forms. Open forms move beyond themselves. They end as often as not on a note of interrogation. They imply more than what is revealed. They have the unclarity of the suggested, the dimly apprehended, the possible. They are difficult because they demand something more of the beholder or the listener than passive appreciation. They demand an active participation of thought and imagination.

Art is perhaps the most accurate reflector of the life of a period, for the artist is in a predominant degree an organism sensitive to the environment. When, therefore, we note in all the arts a movement of revolt against the static and the traditional, and a striving to reveal what the older forms could not compass, we may be sure that this is an expression of what is happening in modern life. We are aware, as we never have been before, of possibility. Reality has for us fluidity, openness. It is both challenge and promise. That is why, although we are in the midst of unprecedented confusion, we are far from being discouraged, but are rather stimulated to find our way to new triumphs of organization. "I tell you," writes Nietzsche, "one must have chaos in one, to give birth to a dancing star." And he adds: "I tell you: ye have still chaos in you."

Contemporary Philosophers

Thus there can be no doubt of what is occurring. A new movement of life is under way. It is not surprising, then, that the spirit of all this should already be in evidence among contemporary philosophers. Hegel made the rather depressing statement that philosophy comes to its conclusions only *after the facts*. "The owl of Minerva takes its flight as the evening shadows begin to fall." He was probably too little impressed with the alertness of the philosophic mind. Today, on the contrary, in one outstanding philosopher after another, we find the forceful expression of points of view in line with these newer trends.

In Whitehead, for example, we discover a definite break with mechanistic views and the formulation of an organismic conception of reality. In Lloyd Morgan and S. Alexander we are given, as over against the entropic philosophy of materialism, the view of a world in which there is a *nisus* toward higher levels of being. In Santayana we find a naturalism that is nevertheless Platonic in spirit; in Woodbridge a realism, not of the particularistic type prevalent in the nineteenth century, but which brings to expression the best of Platonic and Aristotelian universalism. In Dewey we find a realization both of the essential creativeness and the generative interrelations of life. In the soldier-statesman-philosopher, Smuts, we have the reasoned belief, based upon the examination of the scientific processes, of a universe moving toward the development of more widely functioning wholes. In Boodin, Sellars, and Spaulding, we find a philosophy of "creative synthesis." In Montague we discover a stimulating new expression of what he calls a Promethean religion, the religion animated by the spirit of creative innovation and advance.

The movement of philosophy is unquestionably toward the ektropic view. The conception, in short, that reality is a process of self-defeat is one that is at the farthest remove from the most significant philosophic thinking of our day.

Our Philosophy of Life

And so we can dimly perceive the outlines of the new philosophy of life that is doubtless to animate the coming decades of the century. The most powerful and the most meaningful fact to us nowadays is the process of transforming the possibilities of existence into new realities. Life is creative *élan*. It moves away from ignorance, from ineffectiveness, from the futility of a mere repetitiveness. It is an enduring quest for those illuminating truths that enable us to advance to a wider and more significant integration.

Need we then be left with a despairing sense of the complete insignificance of our life? Need we feel crushed before a universe too vast for us to compass? Or worse, in order to signalize our self-respect and our utter veracity, need we stand erect before the omnipotence of that universe and fling it our angry defiance?

The universe, as we now seem to see, is life of our life, spirit of our spirit. It is in us and of us. It moves in all our members. But if this is so, then every creative act we perform, small though it may be, every wish for the more nearly complete, and every will to get it achieved, is our own triumph in a universe that triumphs with us.

INDEX

279

Books that Live

EVERETT DEAN MARTIN
Liberty $3.00
The Meaning of a Liberal Education $3.00
Psychology $3.00
The Behavior of Crowds $3.00
The Mystery of Religion $3.00

BERTRAND RUSSELL
Mysticism and Logic $3.00
Our Knowledge of the External World $3.00
Sceptical Essays $2.50
Philosophy $3.00

H. S. JENNINGS
The Biological Basis of Human Nature $4.00

JOHN COWPER POWYS
The Meaning of Culture $3.00

G. ELLIOT SMITH
Human History $5.00

JOHN B. WATSON
Behaviorism $3.00
Psychological Care of Infant and Child $2.00

H. A. OVERSTREET
About Ourselves $3.00
Influencing Human Behavior $3.00

JOHN DEWEY
Experience and Nature $3.00

FRANZ BOAS
Anthropology and Modern Life $3.00

W · W · NORTON & COMPANY, INC.
70 Fifth Avenue, New York